Also by Frances H. Kakugawa

Mosaic Moon: Caregiving through Poetry

Teacher, You Look Like a Horse:
Lessons from the Classroom

Wordsworth Dances the Waltz

Wordsworth the Poet

The Path of Butterflies

Golden Spike

White Ginger Blossom

Sand Grains

BREAKING THE SILENCE
A CAREGIVER'S VOICE

our voices continue to be heard...
whispered, shouted in silence,
above the din of chaos

Frances Kakugawa

BREAKING THE SILENCE

A Caregiver's Voice

FRANCES H. KAKUGAWA

With additional poetry and journal contributions by

Jason Y. Kimura
Eugenie Mitchell
Linda McCall Nagata
Elaine Okazaki
Red Slider

Willow Valley Press
Nevada City, California

Published by Willow Valley Press, Nevada City, CA

Editing by James Collins and Lynda Straus
Cover by Williams Writing, Editing & Design
Photo of Frances H. Kakugawa by Jason Kimura

www.btsilence.com
www.willowvalleypress.com

The author's proceeds are donated to Alzheimer's Disease International
Marc Wortmann, Executive Director

ISBN: 978-0-9762697-7-9

Library of Congress Control Number: 2010937166

Passages quoted from *Mosaic Moon* by Frances H. Kakugawa

"Jigsaw Puzzle" originally appeared in *The Path of Butterflies* by Frances H. Kakugawa, (Naylor Co. 1976).

Portions of this book are used by permission of and with thanks to the following authors:

Summer Breeze, Jason Y. Kimura, Jody Mishan,
Eugenie Mitchell, Linda McCall Nagata, Elaine Okazaki,
Red Slider, Setsuko Yoshida, Rod Masumoto

"Nightbooks" by Red Slider first appeared, in a different form, in Andrei Codrescu's *Exquisite Corpse* 4, April/May 2000. Used by permission of the author. His poems on Isobel are found in a collection called "Stewards of Mortality" at: http://www.holopoet.com.

Printed in the United States of America
First Edition: November 2010
10 9 8 7 6 5 4 3 2 1

Dedication

This book is dedicated to all my nieces and nephews, who I hope will be the last generation of caregivers for loved ones with Alzheimer's disease. To all the courageous and loving men and women caregivers, and to the equally courageous ones being cared for, I wish I had a magic wand, but since I don't, this book will have to do until there is a cure.

Acknowledgments

I owe so much to the following people and organizations:

To Jason Kimura, Eugenie Mitchell, Linda Nagata, Elaine Okazaki, and Red Slider for their valuable contributions to this book. Their generosity and willingness to go public with their work, so others are able to benefit from their experiences, are immeasurable.

To the Alzheimer's Association chapters throughout the United States, to Mary Gillon and Denise Davis of the Northern California & Northern Nevada Alzheimer's Association and to Elizabeth Stevenson of the Alzheimer's Association-Aloha Chapter, for their commitment to help families in our communities and for their generous support of my work.

To Patricia Lanoie Blanchette, MD, MPH of John Burns School of Medicine, University of Hawai'i, for her medical and humanistic support and knowledge in the field of Geriatric Medecine when my mother was first diagnosed, and for her continuing work today for hundreds of others.

A special acknowledgment to publisher, Barry Schoenborn, for recognizing the need of caregivers to have something besides medicine labels for their daily reading and his faith in my work. To his staff: Jim Collins, Lynda Straus, and Frances Boero, for their professional expertise and patience. It was such a pleasure working with each member of Willow Valley Press.

To Michael Splaine for calling me Sensei [teacher], and for his tireless commitment to the Alzheimer's cause.

To Tim Davis, manager of Peet's Coffee and Tea in Sacramento, California, for providing the haven where I did all my writing over cup after cup of latté in a real cup and for always welcoming me and asking about my writing.

Contents

Foreword

In our aging society, care is the most necessary resource, and the most precious. Will we find—among us as a society and within us as individuals—sufficient capacity to provide the care that will be increasingly needed by our parents, our spouses, our loved ones? And will we find caregivers for ourselves, privileged as we are to live in a time when dying of chronic, degenerative disease is the norm? Cancer, heart and lung disease, and dementia—these are the main story lines in the last chapter of our lives.

Poet and teacher Frances H. Kakugawa answers these question with an echoing, Yes! *Breaking the Silence: A Caregiver's Voice* is a book of enormous hope and transformation. In it we listen to women and men who have mined the vein of care that lies under the surface of our seemingly narcissistic society.

They know that dying, illness, and caregiving are very hard work, and they have discovered that such work can be affirmed by keen observation, self-reflection, and creative written expression.

The terrible reality of Alzheimer Disease is a crucible where this wisdom is hard won, and *Breaking the Silence* shows how resilient Alzheimer caregivers quietly are and how far our system of long-term care still has yet to go in order to support both patients and caregivers in a decent and just way.

The texts in this book are poems, notes, journal entries, and brief commentaries by Kakugawa and five others who have been guided by her in a writing support group process. These texts are intimate, but not idiosyncratic. In them we find facets of a universal human significance—molded by the particular personality, culture, imagination, and sensibility of different individuals.

This is a book about what fundamentally matters—the humanity of caring in the face of dependency and mortality, loss and change, holding on and letting go. This book does more than simply ask us to read; it calls us to reflect.

Bruce Jennings
Director of Bioethics
Center for Humans and Nature
New York, NY

Introduction

This book is a collection of journal stories and poetry written by six present and past caregivers, including me. Our voices tell the story of how we tried to make sense of our unique experiences as caregivers. Our voices are loud, gentle, angry, bewildered, humorous, reflective, and yes, even silent at times. But they are here to be heard by anyone who will listen.

Perhaps the cruelest aspect of Alzheimer's disease and other illnesses accompanied by dementia is that not only do they strip away the memories of our loved ones, they un-write the pages of their history. There is, perhaps, no job more important than to preserve these memories. As caregiver Red Slider wrote, "It was only when I sat down to write and unravel what I saw and felt and heard and touched, that the real meaning of the imprisoned Alzheimer's moment took shape and opened me to what might be hidden in the tiny 'nows' of Isobel's life."

The process is not easy. We often cried openly and without shame on our pages. When I became a caregiver to my mother, I found poetry writing a powerful tool to help transcend the burden of caregiving. It gave voice to almost every aspect of caregiving and led me on a lifelong journey, seeking the divine with profound results and turning my caregiving experiences into resources of creativity, beauty, and peace. It continues to do so now long after the death of my mother. As it was written elsewhere, "In the beginning was the Word." Never do these words seem so true as when we find ourselves helping our loved ones at the end of their lives.

Writing made the difference between a life stuck in the mire of caregiving or living in a world of creative and compassionate freedom, so much so that I extended my own experiences to other caregivers through writing workshops and support groups. These support groups allow caregivers to find channels of expression and ways of saying things that help unravel the chaos of their own experiences. They lend accuracy to observing and reflecting on the behavior and lives of our loved ones, as well as ourselves. And they bring comfort and knowledge.

My book on caregiving, *Mosaic Moon: Caregiving Through Poetry*, told of my first experience working with caregivers. The work then seemed far more raw, untutored, and yes, at times maudlin, in comparison to this book. You may find it curious how the writing in *Breaking the Silence* has evolved from where *Mosaic Moon* left off. One might even think this is the same group of writers/caregivers at a deeper, more practiced level of expression. How did this happen?

 One difference might be that I, myself, was in the midst of battling the agonies of caregiving and struggling right along with the caregivers in my first support group. But with my second and third support groups, whose writings appear here, I was more prepared to guide the participants in exploring the layers of their feelings and meanings a bit deeper. Neither effort can be said to be more successful than the other. These two groups also had their share of Kleenex users and impulsive outbursts. My own evolution in understanding the stages of caregiving, as distinctive as the stages of the disease itself, perhaps made the difference. I am better able to help caregivers understand what was happening to themselves as much as their loved ones. As I evolved, so did the participants in these groups, though they are not all the same people.

Breaking the Silence includes two male caregivers and their work may give answers to the often asked question, "How different are men from women caregivers?"

The poetry and journal stories here cover a broad range of caregivers to loved ones afflicted not only with Alzheimer's disease but with stroke and cancer. Among the six voices of caregivers, you will hear a seventh voice—my own—that evolved as a presenter and analyzer of each caregiver's experiences. While one wouldn't dare add more to a caregiver's voice, for there is really nothing that can be added to their own story, this seventh voice offers some comments on the language itself, on insights I have gained, or on something being said that touched me deeply. *You will recognize this seventh voice in this special font.*

I also added an essay entitled "Two Faces of Alzheimer's Disease" to remind us that there are two people wearing the mask of this disease, the loved ones and the caregivers, and that all the writings in the world change nothing. The progress of the disease will continue and the burdens of the caregiver will only increase over time. Until a cure is found, writing can help us understand the nature of that progress and manage the burdens we bear.

Lastly, during the course of my work with caregivers, I'm often asked, "How do you help people write poetry who claim never to have written anything except grocery lists?" It is possible if one believes as I do, that there is a poet in each of us who wants to be heard. A direct approach to how I open these doors in a support group setting is found at the end of the book. I hope this will prove of value to anyone wanting to start and maintain a writing support group or to any individual just wanting to write. Simply put: meet together, talk story, write, and share the issues and emotions without fear of censorship, and then we can all become learners and teachers. If you are unable to join a support group, then write without one. Writing requires no special tools, only a pen and your voice.

My hope for caregivers is that our poems and stories will give you comfort, help you feel you are not alone, and encourage you to join our voices in preserving the life that must go on during and after caregiving. Only then can we confront this thief that comes into our lives.

For medical and health professionals: Understandably, most of you have neither the time nor resources to deal with more than the pressing demands of your patients and their families. Still, if the stories and poetry in this volume remind you that there is more that may be hidden in the urgent calls for help, then you may discover something more amazing and wonderful, even humorous, in the humanity of caregivers.

Journal and poetry writing may serve as a readily available and always affordable tool that you can suggest your clients might try.

To all readers, thank you.

    Frances H. Kakugawa

Section I:

Poetry and Journal Stories

if the pen, the tongue,
and the heart, filled
the air with one song
of what it means to be human,
what a symphony of truth.

Frances H. Kakugawa

Frances H. Kakugawa

Caregiver for her mother:
Matsue Kakugawa
(1911–2002)

> *i tiptoe softly*
> *in the silence of the house*
> *how loud her absence*

A few days before her death, my mother told Rev. Bruce Nakamura, a Buddhist minister, "Please don't let me be forgotten."

The physical task of caring for her ended with her death, but all other aspects of caregiving and her life go on. They may appear unexpectedly during any hour of the day and night. A thought, an image, a feeling, a dream.

The sound of her voice… it comes like intermittent raindrops and I pause to let them fall across my face. Since her death, my memories turn her into a sage as I recall the lessons I learned from her, words of wisdom I now find myself quoting.

The words "my mother" often precede my sentences. I can almost hear her chuckling over this metaphorical statue I have created in her honor because during my youth, I believed there was nothing she could teach me.

I arrived at a peaceful place, a place not easily found. It took a machete of reflections to help clear a path through the jungle of guilt, remorse, and sadness.

My first poem takes me back to a time and place often viewed as a Do Not Enter zone during caregiving. How can any good daughter wish caregiving to end when it means the death of a loved one? But these unspoken moments came more than once, and when stated in poetic form, it somehow seems permissible to express them without guilt or horror.

Unspoken Mornings

Will lightning strike me down
Before my first thoughts find life?
    How many mornings have I slipped
    Groggily into her room, standing, watching,
    A mother over a crib.
    Her body curled in fetal position,
    Her face toward the wall.
    Still as curtains on a windless day.
    "Is she breathing? Is she alive?
    Is she finally gone, freeing me once again?"
    I continue my sentinel watch.

    "Yes, there is a light stir
    Under her sheet."
    During that split second
    When morning was all stillness
    A sense of relief washed over me

Like cool ocean waves on hot summer days,
Then shameless disappointment
When morning stirred
Into another day. ❦

I had visualized her last moment, her funeral arrangements, all rationally stored in my head, but nothing prepared me for her death. I still want a replay of that scene so I can do it right, with my hand in hers, because it didn't happen that way.

I was not even there, because she drew her last breath after I had left her room. Soon afterward, I was moving like a robot, in a trance, attending to the logistics of death: calls to ministers, funeral parlor, family, and friends.

It also felt brutally final to see or say the words "died" and "death." It seemed gentler to use "passing" or another euphemism, and yet, whatever words I used, I discovered through time that death is not final, for the life that it held is still a process inside of me. Perhaps that life has more staying power than that one second of death. I face both of the "d" words in this poem.

What is Death?

When does a loved one truly die?
I look at her obituary
And it doesn't seem real
To see the word "died"
Next to her name.
Do obituaries tell the truth?

I look at the list of names
Under "In Memoriam"
In Mosaic Moon,
I stop at the date of her death,
I read her name, Matsue Kakugawa
And I wonder, is she really gone?
I take a mental journey through
All the spaces she had filled
And question "What is death?"
Shouldn't my mind, too,
Be purged of all its memories and images,
My heart of all emotional ties?
Shouldn't death also occur
In these parts of me
That still feel her presence?
What is death? ❧

*Sometimes we need to sink ourselves totally into our
solitude to get in touch with ourselves and to allow
silence to resonate in those places where denial or sorrow
have become permanent residents. This silence took
me to the center, where I could give it a name without
being distracted by meaningless chatter. The following
four poems speak of this silence where healing began,
beginning with Sunday afternoons, which seem to hold
more hours than any other day.*

Sundays at 5 P.M.

It is that time,
Whether clocked at Pacific, Eastern
Or Greenwich Mean,
For that relentless ache
To slowly overtake Sunday afternoons,
An ache that has no name,
Just an ache of emptiness,
Unfulfilled dreams and
Unlived moments yet to come.

It is also that time for healing...
A time to smooth jagged edges
Of shattered crystals crunching
Under naked feet.
A time to tweeze each splinter of pain
From broken skin
Of the young and the aged.
It is a time for forgiving...
A time to unlatch doors
Of the caged,
So each can soar to its destination
With messages of peace.

It is a time for solitude,
La Boheme, the blues.
It is, above everything else,
A hell of a time

For being a woman
Who was not born
For Sunday afternoons. 🦑

This poem was written on the sale of my mother's house.
The house where I was born into the hands of a midwife
so many years ago. It speaks of not being able to go home
ever again. The death of both parents no longer gives us a
place to return home to on holidays and special occasions.

This physical change brings new family designs. Who
will replace a parent's home for the holidays? Will this
disintegrate the family that was so important to our
parents? Did we bury our family traditions, folklore, and
myths along with our parents?

Going Home with Thomas Wolfe

my tap root
   no longer
        embraces me...

my tap root
   is slowly fading away ...
        like photos in old albums...

soon,
   that tap root
        will no longer be...

i
    can
        almost
            hear
                its
                    final
                gasp...

"Song of the Wind" was written after I had returned to my mother's house. It had been burned to the ground by the fire department after the new owner had donated it for training recruits. Even without physical evidence, are we not still part of our ancestral roots? The tug of war continues, with my wanting someone to say, "Death does not end."

Song of the Wind

The warrior returns home.
At her feet, ashes, black ashes.
And Silence. Cold Silence.
    Where are the voices
    Of my ancestors?
    Their songs, their stories?

The warrior's cries
Are swallowed by Silence.
A sparrow flies over her head.
    Be still and listen.

A sudden gust of wind
Lifts a fistful of ashes,
Swirls and swirls them
Around her head,
Then over the tangerine trees,
Into the skies.

  Where are the voices
  Of my ancestors?
  Songs of my mother,
  Tales of my grandmother?

A second gust of wind
Lifts another fistful of ashes.
Be still and listen. 🦑

Some things, like Alzheimer's disease and dying, can't be fixed, nor can we control them. But we can try to make some sense of them without any answers if we listen to the silence.

shhh

late summer nights,
over smooth river stones
she strolls barefooted.
her breasts capture
the moon glow as it travels
down to her feet.

hush, be still.
listen to the sound
of silence. 🕸

Soon after my mother's death, I tried to fill the space she had left with activities. One day I began exploring this space I was trying so hard to refill. In exploring that space through poetry, I came to an enlightened discovery. It's alright to grieve. It's all right to preserve and live with that empty space, for it brings in a flowing river, streaming without obstruction. Go to that space, dwell in it until that space is slowly melded into yours as one.

Empty Spaces

Why are we taught since childhood days
To always fill in the spaces?
Before our fingers are able to curl
Around a crayon,
We are given coloring books
To fill in the spaces.
From early childhood we are taught,
Not to stray beyond the lines...
To always fill in the spaces.
All of my life I have lived
With crayons in one hand,
Filling in spaces,
Spaces left by departed lovers, family, friends,
Leaving me crayons smashed against walls
Creating more grief than art.

Today, another space created by her flight.
But this space I will not fill
With any color, stroke or art.
This space bears her name.
To this place I will return time and again,
To be immersed in love, grief, sadness, memories.
This place where all feelings dwell...
No longer a battlefield
Between crayons and me.
This place I will honor and love
For as long as it holds her name. 🦋

There is also the world of dreams where deeply hidden grief is brought to the surface to be reckoned with at the subconscious, and later, conscious level. This dream occurred more than eight years after my mother's death.

A Dream

Last night, my mother died again.
This time, the tears
Eroded and washed down walls
Until there was nothing left,
But remnants of my grief.

There were no tears
The first time she died.
I pulled in the reins,
As I did, all those years,
Caring for her.

I never let go, so afraid
I'd run away
And never be caught.

When she died,
All those years of reining in
Froze the rivers
That wanted free.

She died again last night.
I cried and screamed
All the grief I held.
I tore off the reins
From my flesh
And let the tears
Wash and cleanse
Until morning nudged me
To a new day. ♋

A person brings to caregiving the history of who he or she is. The following story of a caregiver illustrates how cultural upbringing and beliefs, personal values and relationships all congregate one time or another, in caregivers.

Nora, we will call her, was always there and when she said, "I'm dying," I took my pen and kept a journal from that moment on until her last breath. I never imagined a caregiver in my group would face death before her loved one.

This is her story, told through my pen. Whatever I didn't write will have to be found between the lines.

The Scarf

"I have six months to live," she began over the phone, as though her story needed a climactic beginning. "Two weeks ago I was getting dressed to go to Mr. Mishan's funeral when I began having trouble breathing. I went to the ER. They found water in my lungs. The doctor decided to do more tests, so I was kept in the hospital for a week. They found cancer in my ovaries. It's at level four, which means it's very advanced."

She continued her story, pronouncing each word slowly and carefully. "The doctor said it's too advanced for surgery but I could have other treatments. I told him, 'If I have chemo, I know my hair will all fall out. I had a good and long life, so I'm not taking any treatment.' He told me to go home and think about it but I told him I don't need to think about it. I asked him how long do I have and he said six months. He said he never had a patient like me before."

 Oh Nora, I am hearing, I am hearing each word being said. Somewhat clumsily, I interjected with, "I'm so sorry, Nora, what can I do for you?" to which she graciously thanked me by assuring me she was ready to die.

"I feel blessed because now I am given time to clean up our house and get all my papers in order. I'm such a rubbish collector; I need to sort things out."

She concluded this disturbing conversation with, "I started to knit a scarf for you, but I don't think I can finish it in time."

I'm tip-toeing, I'm tip-toeing. "Oh, thank you for thinking of me. Please don't worry about the scarf. Save your energy for your health."

Four years ago Nora walked into my writing support group for caregivers at the Alzheimer's Association library in Honolulu. She came in quietly without a word, nodded her head to me in greeting, put her handbag slowly on the floor, pulled out a chair from under the wooden table, reached down to take out a sheet of paper and pen from her handbag, and sat down. All this was done without a sound, as though any movement or sound she caused would disrupt the room or as if she were taking more than her allowance of space.

She introduced herself and we all had to lean our heads toward her to hear her soft-spoken voice, "I can't write but I came just to listen because I heard Frances speak last month."

I recognized her from a writing workshop I had given to caregivers at Tripler Hospital. She was a tiny woman, less than 4 feet 10 inches, dressed in a light blue *mu'umu'u* with puffed sleeves. She articulated each word slowly as though each word was being processed through her mind before being spoken.

Be patient, be patient, she is teaching you patience… stop running, walk and listen.

I turned into a broken record each time she shared a story, "Nora, write that down."

Nora felt comfortable speaking in Japanese. Often with encouragement, she wrote in both Japanese and English. Her Japanese captured what English lost in translation.

She was a caregiver for her father and then her parents-in-law. Now, she was caring for her elderly mother who was over 100 years old.

"Last week the neighbors called the police at 3 o'clock in the morning because they heard me yelling at my mother." In elegant Japanese, she repeated what she had shouted to her mother. Her Japanese was not vernacular, "Mother, I don't know what to do anymore because I am so tired. If you don't go to bed, I won't be able to sleep." Oh neighbors, if only you understood Japanese, you would have heard Nora use the honorific dialect which signaled respect, love, and honor toward her mother with a hearing problem.

Nora was married to a World War II veteran who had been a prisoner in a German town until the end of the war. They were both second generation Japanese Americans.

"My husband is the typical samurai. He doesn't tell me how he feels about things. He's happy as long as I cook and take care of him. But I want to travel; I want to take a cruise, but he won't go.

"When he was a prisoner, he was kept in a house with a family. The family was very nice to him. Last week we got a letter from the daughter, who was just a child when my husband was there. Her parents are now gone. I told my husband we should go to Germany and thank this family but he said, 'What for? He won't talk about the war.'"

Nora was a product of first-generation Japanese parents who raised her according to strict Japanese cultural mores. Her father kept a daily journal in Japanese, which became his means of educating Nora. When I pushed Nora to write, she confessed, "I don't like to write because my father used to sit me down and read his journal to me. He did this when I did something improper or wrong. I just hated to sit and listen to him."

She was raised to believe a woman took care of her husband and children with gratitude. She shared this:

"My mother always told me to accept life as it is. All suffering is my fate for being a woman. On the day I got married, my mother told me:

> *Sekai de ichibun hitori musume,*
> *Kawai watashi no hitori go Michiko,*
> *Takeshi san to nakayoku tanoshiku,*
> *Sugoshi nasai ne.*
> *Kodomo tachi kawai-i gattai ne*
> *Okasan inoote ilu yo.*

> "In this whole wide universe, I have only one child, my adorable daughter called Michiko. Marry Takeshi and have a loving life with him. Be one with him in heart. I will be waiting to see adorable children someday."

Nora struggled with guilt. She felt she was dishonoring all that her parents taught her about filial piety when she placed her mother in a private nursing home. Encouraged to write a letter to her mother, she wrote in formal Japanese,

> "Forgive me, mother, for being such an ungrateful daughter. I put you in this care home because I cannot take care of you anymore. I don't visit you every day. I didn't visit you on your birthday last week because it hurt me too much to see you as you

are today. Please forgive me. I am such an ungrateful daughter."

Not long after her mother's death, she became a caregiver for her husband. "This is my lot in life. I was born to take care of others. I should be happy I can take care of him. If I think this way, I don't feel so bad."

And yet, the subject of a cruise came up again and again. It was her dream cruise. Oh Nora, I wish I could put wings on you and let you fly with freedom. Subtly, subtly, I come in the back door with my poems written for her:

Nisei Woman

I am generations of women
Looking in at layers of silk kimonos,
Muffled giggles, *koto* movements,
Knowing they can only be
Mere images of desire.
I am generations of women
Waiting to be dragonfly wings,
A maple leaf, spiraling snowflake,
A cherry blossom,
Released and detached from
Generations of cultural clasps.

I am generations of women,
Suppressed in thin *yukata*
Stuck ankle deep in rice fields,

Scarecrows on wooden stakes.
Denied, yet desiring wantonness
Beneath layers of silk.
I am woman,
Suppressed,
Dying. ✿

[Nisei: second generation Japanese-American]
[Koto: Japanese stringed instrument that resembles a zither]
[Yukata: cotton kimono]

"I am Japanese and this is my lot," echoed Nora over and over again. I wrote this poem after taking a few lessons in Japanese flower arrangement. "Here, Nora," I said, "Take off your kimono if it's stifling you."

Three Ikebana Lessons
Lesson #1

From *sensei* (teacher):
"Conceal the front rim of the vase
With fern or flowers.
The front is not seen
Just as a woman
Keeps the front of her kimono
Closed, by taking tiny steps."
    "Yes, Sensei."
    I bow to the sensei.
    I am obedient. ✿

Lesson #2

"We do not worry about the back of the vase.
Ikebana is placed against the wall.
Only front matters."
>Hmmm ... was I raised to be an Ikebana?
>
>Always show saved face?
>
>Do not expose what is not seen?
>
>This is being Japanese?
>
>Yes, smile?
>
>Bow, be nice?
>
>Let no one know
>
>What weeps deep inside?
>
>Desires, needs, dreams?
>
>No, only front matters?
>
>Keep buried, like samurai swords
>
>And Japanese porcelain dolls
>
>After Pearl Harbor, Hiroshima?
>
>Yes, smile, be nice?
>
>Only front matters? ❧

Lesson #3

"Ah, maybe put orange flower
In the back, behind yellow protea.
Good to see little color from back."
>No! No more shadowing.
>
>Let my voice entombed
>
>For generations break the silence
>
>Of the Buddhist hall.

I am not Ikebana.
I am not merely heaven, man and earth
Rooted by cultural hands.
Sift those sands. Yes!
I am free!
I am tossed into the winds.
I shed my kimono.
I spread my legs.
I am free. ✌

A few months into our sessions, Nora began to arrive with
a twinkle in her eye and a soft smile on her face, saying, "I
went to my first matinee movie by myself. Thank you for suggesting it, Frances. I heard your voice encouraging me."

And then, "I went to a health conference at the hotel in
Waikiki. I stayed overnight and took a room and I felt good
eating in a restaurant by myself. I asked my husband to join
me but he didn't want to, so I went by myself."

Then later, "Thank you for the McDonald's and Starbucks
gift certificates. I took a bus to Starbucks after our session
last month and had a cup of café mocha just as you suggested. It was so good. I enjoyed being there by myself. I
didn't have to worry about anyone."

Slowly, slowly, I saw the loosening of the bonds that held
Nora tightly. Yes, I thought, take larger strides; it will take
you there faster and sooner.

Her husband began to need more care, while her lifelong
dream of going on a cruise dimmed. "My husband can't travel

anymore because he's in a wheelchair and needs to be near a bathroom. Now, I'll never go on that cruise."

"Nora," I said, "Take a cruise by yourself. You can do that." and she said, "Yes, you're right. Someday I will."

One night, after being in our support group for almost a year, she invited her husband to watch her take a shower. "I asked him if he wanted to see me take a shower. Luckily, his wheelchair was able to fit through the bathroom door, and for the first time in our married life, he saw me naked. He seemed to enjoy it, even if he didn't say anything." Nora had been married for almost fifty years.

Ah, Nora, don't you see, you are on a cruise right now. You are sailing with wings on your feet. Look at you now.

P. O. Box
Hawai'i, USA

I am... gasping... for... breath
This box that once spelled home
Suddenly closes in on me,
Constricting my breath.
My legs and arms entangled
In cultural webs of myths and lore
From ancestral lands,
Eulogized with social rules:
How I should live, Who I should be,
What is right, What brings shame?
One way or the other, freezes me into ice.
This self, created by years of containment

Fashioned for the public will
Now threatens to burst free.
I have become a truth that doesn't exist
Outside of this box. Oh life!
Contaminate me! Strip off my white robe,
My robe of air-tight alibis,
Formulas on how to be, a social perfection.
Oh, strip me good.
Wrap your blanket full of holes
With wildness of life, around my naked body,
Let me slush around in the sewers of your life
Right up to my open wounds to suck it dry.
Take me. Take me
Where freedom without judges
Is the ensign of my existence.
Now, Life! Before I am too dead. ❧

Nora continued to loosen her kimono. One morning she
brought in an article on how both music and learning new
things improve the minds of the elderly. With encouragement and permission, Nora began piano lessons, fulfilling
a secret desire from her youth. Her lessons led her into her
first recital. An aura of joy developed around her. She walked
at a faster pace, spoke with fewer pauses, and her voice
vibrated with life. The sparkle in her eyes could no longer be
hidden behind her Japanese fan.

I smiled the day she called me to say, "I have a crush on my
piano teacher. He's younger than me but I like him. He's so
kind and helps me so much. I can't believe I feel all this for
him. I feel like a young girl."

"Nora! There's hope for you. I'm so happy to hear this."

"You're not going to lecture me on how silly I am, that I'm an old lady and shouldn't have crushes like this?"

"Nora, isn't it a wonderful place to be, to feel such joy, such excitement? Some people go through life unable to feel so strongly. Count this as a blessing."

"Thank you for saying all this. I don't plan to do anything about these feelings; it's just good to have them. This is why I look forward to my lessons. I don't play that good but he's so kind to me."

Some months later she called. "I'm sort of depressed. My piano teacher is moving his studio to the other side of the island and referred me to another teacher. I don't think I'll continue my lessons."

"Nora," I consoled, after suggesting she see her physician for her depression, "It's okay to continue your feelings for your teacher. Just flow with it. I do wish you'd continue your lessons with the new teacher. You enjoy the music you play and who knows, Nora, your new teacher might turn into a bigger crush."

She laughed, "The new teacher is a woman."

A few weeks later her voice reclaimed the joy it seemed to have lost. "I told my doctor what you said and he agreed with you. So, I'm taking lessons from this woman. He gave me some medication for my depression. He also said I must continue this support group because it's good for me." She continued her lessons until caregiving took this time away from her.

"Frances," she proudly told me one day, "I bought a computer and my husband and I are taking lessons. I decided I'm not too old to learn new things. Now I can email you after you move to Sacramento." And she did for two years.

～

Three weeks after being diagnosed with cancer, she moved into a private care home to be under the care of the Hospice Program. She told me, "I don't want to die at home because some cultures don't like to buy houses where someone died in it and someday, if my husband and sons want to sell this house, I want them to be able to sell it. So, coming to this home is perfect. And Frances, I'm still trying to work on your scarf."

"Nora, send me the scarf even if you don't finish it. I want it because you're making it."

"But you'll choke on it if I don't finish it," she laughed. "It can hardly go around your neck right now."

"Oh, I can hang it on the wall like a piece of art. Or I can choke on it each time I use it."

～

On Christmas Day I asked her, "How are you feeling, Nora? Do you feel lonely at nights when everyone's asleep? What do you think about before you fall asleep?"

"No, I don't feel lonely. I'm just looking forward to being with God. It's not that easy to die. I wear Depends now."

"I am so blessed. Elaine comes to visit me. I got a card from Jason and Linda. My husband is in denial and still thinks I'm going home. I asked him to come stay with me here but he said he'll feel more comfortable at home."

"My sons hug me and I feel so loved. Before I left home, my son saw your poetry books in the boxes and he asked if he could have them. I felt good that he wanted your books. My mother died so peacefully and I thought it would be that way for me, too. It's not easy to die."

"Nora, you have taken care of all the details of your dying. Maybe you need to spend the rest of your time on living instead of dying."

"Oh, what wisdom," she responded, gasping for breath.

"Elaine visited me today and when she left I thought, 'I may never see her again,' but I need to say, 'I will see Elaine again. Yes, I will.' Thank you."

"Nora, I'm going to Hawai'i in March to give a talk. I'm going to see you then."

"Before today, I would have said I'll be gone by then. But today, I'm going to say, I will see you in March. That's only the fourth month so I will see you. I'll live until then."

"And Nora, remember that scarf? I want to wear that scarf. Finish it for me."

"I have seventeen more inches to knit and if I do one inch a day, maybe I can finish it in time."

∽

Nora's firstborn son was killed at age three when a car hit him while he was riding his tricycle. Nora was giving birth to her second son in the hospital when the accident happened. To protect Nora from grief, a family decision was made to have burial services before she returned from the hospital with her newborn son.

"I never got to see my son again."

❧

Her youngest son had been missing for years somewhere on an island in the Pacific. Hired investigators had been unsuccessful in locating him. "I guess I'm going to die without seeing him. This makes me sad. I gave birth to four sons and I have only two now."

❧

Her voice no longer sounded light and upbeat. She was using oxygen and her pain was managed with morphine, although she didn't mention her pain at all.

"So many people want to help me but I've never received help like this before. I was the one taking care of others all of my life. It's hard for me to accept help."

"Nora, let others care for you now. When someone wants to do something for you, you need to let them do this because when you receive, they too, are receiving, and you can't deny that gift to others. It's a two-way gift. When I send something to you, it's for me, too. It's my way of telling you I love you. And this is all I can do from here."

"Thank you. Yes, you are right. I won't stop friends and family who want to help me. It's my turn now."

❧

Nora often spoke of wanting to be free as a bird. "When I'm stuck in traffic, I used to tell my husband, 'I wish I could be a bird so I can just fly over all the cars and be on time for my appointment.' I told my husband to release colorful pigeons at the end of my funeral service but he said it's too much of a problem."

"This is about Nora, not you!!! Get those pigeons!!!" I angrily thought to her husband.

I sent her a set of glass bird ornaments that move and sparkle in light. "Nora, I bought myself the same set of birds and every Christmas I'll be putting them on my tree and you will be here in memory. I'm telling you this because I want you to know what's going to happen after you're gone. You will not be forgotten."

She responded with silence followed by a soft "Thank you."

〜

Ah, Nora, bless you for leaving all doors open, even one for my feeble attempt at being ha-ha funny.

"Nora, I expect you to come to greet me when it's my turn to die. And I expect a mink-covered recliner waiting for me. You've got to arrange that when you're in heaven. I'll try to live a good life till then." She managed to laugh despite her constant coughing.

〜

"Frances, I guess I'm not going to take that dream cruise after all. I told the care home owner to bag all my clothes and send them home. I don't need much. And don't send me anything anymore."

"Nora, maybe you're taking the ultimate cruise which is the cruise to heaven."

"A cruise to heaven. I like that."

〜

Our conversations were now brief, "Nora, I love you. You are a gift to me. Thank you."

"I love you, too, and thank you for being my friend. I'm so blessed. I'm so lucky."

I sent her the following poem to which she responded, "I don't deserve all these words."

Nora

you are that lotus blossom
rising above the murky waters
lifting its face toward
the morning sun.
you are that first crocus
seeking its way
out of the cold icy ground
the magic that is spring.
you are that sunflower
searching for light
in the midst of summer
for all its glory.
you are a raindrop
on desert plains
bringing magic, wonder
on arid soil.
you are the painted hills
fiery in all their brilliance
awaiting the first fall
of winter's splendor.
you are wings in flight
over freeways, cities,

mountains, bridges,
and ships on sea.

you are all seasons,
vines into grapes
grapes into wine
journeying without end.
thank you, my friend
for the lessons taught,
lessons lived
of how it is to be born,
to live, to die and to live
once again in every season
for life eternal. 🪷

I sent manuscripts of my two children's books to Elaine to
be read to Nora on a good visit. They will be published after
her predicted six months. Nora was at most of my book
signings, poetry readings, and workshops open to the public
during these past four years. I'd look out into the audience
and there she'd be, smiling, dressed in her colorful *mu'umu'u*
and a flower in her hair. No small accomplishment as Nora
made her way to newly-found freedom on crowded city buses.
There were days when she walked in with an umbrella, her
hair wet with raindrops.

~

I called Nora to wish her a happy new year. I found myself
reciting the traditional formal Japanese greeting, bowing my
head in respect. I left the second line of the greeting unsaid
because for a split second, the thought of speaking of life in

the new year didn't seem appropriate. When she whispered hello, I said, "Nora, this is Frances. *Ake-mashite, Omedeto-gozaimasu.*"

Through her labored breathing she slowly returned the following greeting in a formal recitative voice, pausing to catch her breath, reciting syllable by syllable:

Ake-mashite-Omedeto-gozaimasu.

Konnen mo, yoroshiku onegai shimasu.

"Yes," I managed, moved that she completed the greeting asking me with deep humility, to continue our relationship in the newly awakened year.

Shifting her voice to more casual language, she added, "I thought I was going to die last night but I'm still here today. I'm going to work on your scarf when I'm feeling better. It's not turning out nice. I'm running out of yarn and I don't want to bother my son to get me more."

~

"Call Nora," I thought. I was rushing out to my doctor's appointment and thought, "Later, I'm late." "Call Nora" entered my thoughts again. I put my handbag down and called Nora. When I heard the care home owner Jane's voice, I knew there were changes since my last call.

"Frances, we're going to lose Nora. We thought we lost her yesterday. She will probably be gone by the end of today."

"Can she take my call? Is she conscious?" I asked.

"Yes."

She put the phone next to her ear. I asked "Nora?" after hearing shuffling sounds in the background. Jane came on the telephone again.

"Nora just expired as I put the phone to her ear."

"Nora."

I lit a red candle for a few minutes, and then drove out to my appointment. A few blocks before the medical center, five birds appeared in front of my car. One bird separated from the rest and slowly dipped and soared three times, wings wide apart, then joined the flock and they were gone. Her scarf arrived a few weeks later and as expected, it was red.

I continued to be the voice for others who often found intense emotions obstructing their way. This poem came to me in bright visuals while listening to a caregiver's story of her sisters' interest in their mother's finances and their refusal to get involved in their mother's care. The caregiver's "but we are sisters" expressed her confusion and grief.

across crayoned fields

Today … only **black, white and gray**…
Parched wastelands of humanity
Barren, sizzling in hot summer.
Black vultures circling above,
Waiting for a last breath…
White porcelain faces of sisters
Uttering their inability to become human…

Gray where hope, prayer and beliefs
In human goodness linger
For half a second
Before dissipating into the reality
Of what is. **Black. White.** ✦

*After the death of my mother, questions of my own
mortality began to preoccupy my thoughts. Each year I
took each birthday to mean a step closer to death. "Will
I be next?" If a test were available to predict the onset of
Alzheimer's disease, would I take it? I reflect on these
thoughts on aging and of being the next victim in the next
two poems. Sometimes, it's best to turn to your funny bone
for the unanswerable as I did in "Who Will Be the Me for
Me?"*

Who Will be the Me for Me?

*[Iris is writer Dame Murdoch, and John is her husband,
John Bayley]*

Matsue had me,
Iris had John,
Ronnie had Nancy,
Who will I have
When I grow old?
My options are many
So I never lose sleep
On who will be me for me.

Option One:

    I will find a younger man

    Many springs to my autumn.

    A nurse's aide, preferably

    Like young Ernesto at

    My mother's care facility.

Option Two:

    I will sacrifice my original plan

    Hanging around country clubs for wealthy men,

    But will stick to nurses' lounges

    At UC Davis Medical or Kaiser Permanente,

    Find not one but a dozen friends

    All young, crisp RN's.

Option Three:

    I will go to South Carolina

    Where prisons cater to Alzheimer's inmates,

    Those lifers have aged without parole.

    I'll rob a bank in that city

    Be housed forever in their Alzheimer's section

    With murderers, rapists, and terrorists,

    All without memory.

Which will it be?

    My first would be an Ernesto

    Who'd be strong with wheelchairs and Hoyer lifts.

    With our language barrier, he won't hear

All my vulgarity in Japanese.
I will be speaking Japanese, won't I?
But if all fails, I'll return
To the most sensible, already in print:
A long-term care insurance,
A nursing home under Frances Tapat,
A health directive
And God as my Me. ✤

Knock, Knock, Who's There?

We joke and laugh at my many exits.
"Bye," I say, "I'm off to the post office."
The door slams. Soon I'm back again.
"I forgot to take my letters."
He hears the slamming of the door again
And again and again.
Is it another exit or entrance?
How many goodbyes before I finally leave?
We joke and laugh
But there's that shadow
Draped in black that lurks
Somewhere in my laughter.
Yesterday I stood in the kitchen.
"What am I looking for? Why did I come?"
My brain squeezed shut, I walked out
Empty-handed.

I search for 10 Across

"ID theft target" in NY Times crossword puzzle.
The digging, deeper, the fog, denser.
"It'll come, just go on to 12 Down."
Has the shadow found its way
Through the door left ajar?
"I'm home," I say, slamming the door.
"I'm home." ❧

Slowly approaching the age of one's own parents brings unsettling speculation that perhaps time is running out. The hands of the clock can't be turned back. We need to embrace age and celebrate our life span in the here and now, as we did in our youth.

winds of the young

how regrettable to be almost all-knowing, matured
and wise.
after decades of life, how very disheartening
to be so cemented to one's own existence,
that sense and reason become the forum
for all who come, those unexpected guests
from the back alleys of my youth.

oh, but to be there once again,
whipped by the winds, back and forth and any which
way.
to be that kid facing the world
believing life is for saying yes, yes, yes,
to doors left open for the welcome or the leave.

how lamentable to have come to this stage in life,
so locked and rooted in one's own reality.
how utterly mortifying to be so wizened with age,
one begins each day aware of consequences
instead of edges.
ah, but to be irrepressible, unafraid,
tossing caution to the winds,
ah yes, I was there so many times:
it was there my heart got broken
and my poetry got written,
I flew with wings,
without feet or sense
of the ground.
why did I ever grow up?
or did I grow old?

Retirement and care homes are sprouting in all parts of our world, a physical response to the problem of caring for our long-living family members. Science and technology continue to extend life expectancies. My father died at age 59 from cancer in 1963, saying he had outlived his own father so he had lived a good life. My mother died at age 90 in 2002. As each generation outlives the older, longevity brings problems that are not always solvable by the sciences responsible for its creation.

How to care for our elderly involves issues beyond affordable physical structures for them. At first glance, this seems plausible and uncomplicated. In actuality, it quickly becomes complicated because removing loved ones from a familiar environment, away from family and friends and placing them into a new lifestyle, has serious consequences. Such environments are easier for the young than the elderly, who do not easily adapt to new and strange surroundings. Something seems to be reversed here. Decisions to place a loved one in a retirement or care home are often based on practicality and necessity more than the heart, much to the sorrow of caring family members. I look into the thoughts of families in this next poem after visiting a friend in a new retirement home.

Noh Drama

[Noh Drama is a Japanese stage play using masks.]

On a quiet Saturday evening,
I join my friend in the dining room
Of her residence in a new retirement home,
Advertised as one of the most plush residences
In the city.

I sit and watch porcelain masks:
On a man in a wheelchair,
On two women slow dancing the shuffle
Led by their walkers,
A couple gingerly entering the room,
Not as debonair Englishmen,
But simply, two old men with canes.
A few join visiting family members
For the last supper of the day.

All with porcelain masks,
Smiling at their grown children
Also masked in smiles.

I can almost hear
Their voices of affirmation:
Yes, this was the right thing to do.
Everyone is happy, happy.
Freedom not to cook, clean or scrub,
Freedom not to water their flowers,
Or dine from their garden.
Freedom not to live
In houses etched with memories.
Yes, this was the right thing to do.
Freedom.

After supper, they wait silently for the elevator.
What do they do after the doors close?
What do they do in their rooms?
Do they take their masks off
At their doors and lay them aside?
Or do they go to bed masked,
Hoping to become one with each painted smile?
I should have ordered dessert. ❧

*In Mosaic Moon, I have a poem titled "Dear Caregiver,"
expressing the other voice, that of a loved one asking to be
in a nursing facility to unburden family members.*

My own mortality continues to surface. Did my mother, too, reflect on her own aging? Why don't we take a razor and scrape away labels that spell "elderly," "seniors," or "old"? Imagine my shock when I realized numbers were now going to make a great difference in my life after age 65, especially in doctor's offices. It was no longer my mother's milieu but mine.

The young doctor (and why do they all look so young these days?), looked at my birth date before asking me why I was there.

"Oh," she said, "You don't look your age."

After I told her the details of all the pain I was experiencing, she said, "Seems like you still have a few good years left, so I'll give you this prescription." A prescription without even touching her stethoscope to my heart? A prescription without even knowing the cause of my pain? Do young doctors know magic?

To my question, "What will this prescription do?" she responded, "It'll stop your brain from sending pain to your body."

"No," I said, "I can stand this pain. I need to know the cause of this pain before getting a prescription." She insisted on the prescription, so I took it and left it in the trash can on my way out. Besides, my ten-minute office visit was up.

Aside from feeling angry and insulted (don't medical schools teach students that calling a woman old is worse than bird flu?), I felt very sad that these young doctors see the elderly as people who don't deserve medical diagnosis.

I didn't have the time or interest to tell her I have more than a few good years left working with the elderly and sick, helping them with respect, love, compassion and dignity. I continue to learn incredible life lessons from each of them. I didn't tell her this. She didn't hear me when I told her I had pain; why would she hear me now?

The next poem speaks to those who see the elderly as having lived out their lives by age 65 and who believe that only productivity in the workplace has human worth. Yes, Dylan Thomas, I am once again raging against the dying of the light.

On Becoming 69

How can I be 69 when I feel 49?
How can my mother's daughter turn 69?
For God's sake, children aren't supposed to age.
Not children born out of mothers' wombs.
How can my mother's daughter turn 69?

Four years ago, it all began...
They called me elderly,
Neatly categorized under OLD.
They began mailing me funeral plans,
Nursing home ads on slick colored sheets
In large black print.
They gave me flu shots before anyone else,
Invitations to free luncheons
By long-term care insurance agents.

"You are dying," their messages said.
Shall I tell them of my 88th birthday
When I plan to make love and hear the leaves move
On a windless day? 🦋

When I am 88

When I am 88
I will have a love affair

That will leave me trembling
On a windless day.
I will drown in Puccini,
Mozart, Verdi.
Tidal waves roaring
Inside of me.

I will feel the brush strokes
Of Van Gogh,
Clawing, bleeding
My inner flesh.

I will be Shakespeare
Vibrant, on stage,
Rivers rushing, splashing
Over moss and stone.
I will become soft,
Sensuous, wet

Against your skin,
Silk against steel.

When I am 88
I will still be woman,
Yes! ❧

Too often we conclude that a person is not present unless speech and memory are present, eyes opened and visual responses observable. I've heard so many family members say. "They no longer know me so I don't visit them anymore." But, synapses believed to be permanently disconnected can mysteriously link and the person thought to be gone reappears, as I experienced on many occasions.

Perhaps if we take away our fear of the unknown and embrace what is not known, we will be able to accept a final gift, transforming us into the most humanitarian of all beings.

The elderly, even in their dementia, offer lessons unimaginable, as seen in the following story and two poems.

Isogaba Maware

A few ladies looked alert instead of wearing their usual distant looks. Even Mrs. Kono, 101 years old, whose voice I had not yet heard, extended both hands out to me in greeting.

"Why not?" I decided and chatted away about my morning before arriving in the solarium where lunch was being served.

"I got up early this morning to register for my yoga class. I wanted to be there early to be sure I would have a space in class. I knew I would have to wait half an hour before registration so I brewed myself a cup of decaf coffee, adding chocolate, sugar and hot milk. Just as I was putting the lid on, a tiny roach appeared on the counter so I reached over to smash the roach. Instead, I knocked my cup of coffee all over the counter, floor, and on my white shorts."

My mother chuckled softly with an amused look on her face. "She heard me," I thought in delight.

Mrs. Ito laughed and said in Japanese, "Isogaba maware."

Another woman chuckled, nodded and said, "Isogaba maware."

She and Mrs. Ito began to discuss the original saying and decided Mrs. Ito's version was correct.

I asked Mrs. Ito for a translation and using both arms to demonstrate a circle, she explained, "When one rushes, instead of going in a straight line, one goes in a circle." I repeated after her and wrote it down. I thanked her for teaching me something so beautiful and meaningful.

Mrs. Ito suffers from Alzheimer's disease, and before her lunch was over, she was back into her own world of silence. I stayed to spoon-feed the ladies and remain in their quiet company.

Later, as I walked to my car, I felt uplifting joy for the lesson learned that they are still there, oh yes, they are still there.

Listen to my mother's two words. Even in her dementia state she recognizes insincerity and knows when a member of the nursing staff is being condescending. In our multi-cultural society, there's a need for the medical profession to include cultural beliefs and practices in their medical knowledge base so human dignity will be honored and respected.

On the other hand, there is also a need to educate people whose cultural or spiritual beliefs create conflict and confusion within them when confronted with the science of medical care. There are many double edges to life which need to be sorted out for the good of the patient.

Plastic Orchids

"Matsue, I love you.

Matsue, I love you."

The Aide sing-songs to my mother,

As she lifts her

Out of her wheelchair.

"Bull shit," I hear my mother say.

"Bull shit," once again, quietly

To herself but I hear her

From the doorway of her room.

Yes, bullshit. In her generation

No one calls her Matsue except

Older siblings, her husband, parents.

Everyone else bestows respect with

"Matsue-san."

A stranger calling her Matsue

And vowing love

Is as genuine as a stem

Of plastic orchids.

To believe that communication needs spoken words is to be deprived of some of life's most treasured lessons. The elderly, without voice, speak volumes with their eyes and body movements. Listen to my dialogues with 102-year-old Mrs. Kono, who doesn't speak at all.

Dear Mrs. Kono

For one and a half years
She watched me quietly
As I visited my mother.
At age 102, she had no visitors.
She spoke not a word
But her eyes, so clear
Observed everyone in her midst.
She'd extend her hand for a shake
Or nod to me at my greeting.
But she somehow knew,
I was there for my mother.

Today, I visited her floor.
She took my hand
And held it tightly
And wouldn't let go.
"Do you remember me?"
I asked in Japanese.
She nodded, nodded, nodded nonstop,
Her fingers curled tightly into mine

As if a lifeline ran between us.
Her eyes filled with tears
When I kissed the top of her head.
And still she clenched on.
Somehow she seems to know.
My mother is no longer here.
Somehow she seems to know,
I now have time and space
To love her as my own. ❧

Past, present, and future: At one point in our lives, they all converge and we can't deny or ignore any of these stages, can we? I tried to turn my back to a future that spelled "old," but over a cup of latté I learned to embrace all the stages of life.

2-1/2 Inch High Heels

I sit at Kahala Mall,
Starbucks latté
In my hand.
A parade of seniors walk pass
With canes, walkers, wheelchairs
While those who walk alone
At snail's pace
Are held by partners.
I look at my 2-1/2 inch heels
And close my eyes
To this parade

That continues to pass
Before me.
Who gave them permission
To rob me of this time
With my latté?

They have no song, no drums,
No batons twirling to beat...
Only a silent message
That this is life...
Life when 2-1/2 inch heels
Will someday be traded in
For canes, walkers, wheelchairs,
My arm held by someone younger.
Are they reminiscing
Of a time when they, too,
Once walked in heels
2-1/2 inches high?

I leave my latté
On the coffee table,
Join them around the mall.
One fragile hand tightly holds mine.
It doesn't matter who's
Walking whom when
We're at the mall.

Holidays are difficult times. I replaced "grief" with
"celebration" because when I think of grief, I feel I must

grieve. Celebration brings me laughter and quiet moments of joy. This is one of my celebrations during the holidays.

Playtime with a Memory

This was a mother-daughter game we played before she was diagnosed with Alzheimer's disease. During Christmas, I would purchase a sweater or a dress or a piece of jewelry and ask my mother, "Hey Okasan, you want to buy this for my Christmas present?" and she would always laugh and say, "What? You can't buy it for yourself when you have a good job? Sure, I'll buy it for you if you're not ashamed to take your poor mother's money." And no matter what price I quoted, her answer would always be, "Only that much?" and she'd hand me the cash.

This past Christmas, I saw a beautiful woolen black and red scarf, highly priced at Nordstrom's and felt it was too extravagant. Then I silently asked, "Hey Okasan, how about buying this for me for Christmas?" I'm still waiting to receive her check.

Many Alzheimer patients turn to babbling in later stages of the disease. These next two poems pose the question, "Have we thought that maybe we are the ones with language deficiency?" Perhaps if we learn to see through their eyes and hear through their ears, we will learn more of their world instead of being stuck in our own. This may lead us to find a way to caregive with less conflict and to find answers to the question, "Which of us lives in a normal world?"

Babblelese

Babbling...
sounds without words
a soliloquy on stage
her eyes on fire
her head nodding with passion
periods commas disappear her babbling
Continues chuckles laughter...
We speak our French, Italian,
English and even Japanese,
but no one, no one
has taught us Babblelese.
Why so much laughter in Babblelese?
Are all her secrets being released
Riding the winds on whose wings they fly?
Babblelese -
Language reserved
For the precious few. ৩৯

Misdiagnosis

Another misdiagnosis:
Hey Doc, she ain't got no language
Perception decay.
She's merely turning into a poet,
A literary jewel of metaphors,
A perceiver of images unseen
By passers-by, medical tests and research.

Ah, Doc,
Blessed are the poets
Born daily into our lives. ♋

Caregivers find their lives gradually being put on hold as their energy and hours become totally consumed by their mission. Often, the self put-on-hold is no longer present after caregiving, and a new, re-invented self demands to reenter the circle of life once again. I stopped golfing and flute lessons during caregiving and later found it difficult to return.

Caregiving is a powerful tool to change one's own personal sense of values. To take a journey with someone on the edge of their life is to learn what it means to be human. This may be the ultimate result of being caregivers, going through a transformation that takes time and effort. I have seen caregivers struggle to resume life as it was before, and feeling stuck because that life was past and the person who lived it was no longer here.

looking out my window

three robins pecking in unison
on freshly mowed lawn,
it must be spring.
crepe myrtle displaying naked limbs
wrapped in emeralds and jades.
rosemary shooting blossoms
in lavender and pinks,
green turtle basking on a rock

in a fish pond.
yes, it must be spring
my feet, still frozen in last winter's slush,
paralyzed. is it truly spring? ✿

*In this final poem I speak of those ordinary acts that
become extra-ordinary after one is deprived of them during
caregiving years.*

and yet, and yet ...

now there are sunday mornings
of crossword puzzles
filled in one sitting...
invitations rsvp'ed in ink,
spur of the moment outings
to theaters and malls...
conversations with adults:
an art once lost, best selling novels
beginning to end...
no late fees
on credit card bills,
or unsent Christmas cards in May...
time and self again,
in the river that keeps flowing
in loss and relief. ✿

Frances H. Kakugawa
Sacramento, California

Elaine Okazaki

Caregiver for her Mother:
Natsuyo Kojima
(1911 – 2006)

I was a poor caregiver model for Elaine. I taught with Elaine at the same school for four years. She once invited me to her class of first graders as a poet, to help her students write haiku poems.

When I heard her mother was diagnosed with Alzheimer's disease, I invited Elaine to our once-a-month support group. It was months later that she appeared. Her reason why it took her so long to join us is explained in the following note she e-mailed to members of the support group:

> It took me a while to attend the support group because being Japanese, I didn't want anyone to know. If anyone hears I'm going to a support group, I'd be embarrassed. Support group connotes weakness, needy. Once I came, I was so glad... it was a place to go to on Saturdays. I felt such a void when Frances left.

I say I was a poor model for Elaine because when she first attended our session, she confessed observing my mother and me, walking the mall slowly and peacefully with my mother's hand in mine, and she fantasized doing the same with her mother someday. "It was such a loving sight," she said.

But it was not going to be, because her mother chose to follow a different drummer at the mall. When Elaine came to her first session, feeling frustrated and indignant because her mother was not like my mother, I laughed, appreciating her mother's own feisty personality, and soon Elaine learned to laugh with me.

Elaine, in her honesty, allows us a peek into how support groups and the writing process work in transforming us into more knowledgeable and compassionate caregivers. Her poems show how she used whatever coping skills were available to her at the time of a crisis. That little voice that says "write" led her to reflect, explore, and search for the right words and voice. When she returned to the crisis with her poem, some of the frayed edges were smoothed and buffed. Sharing her poems with others, she received support, laughter, and more insights into what was truly happening in her mother's mind.

Elaine taught me this, that there can be no formula or norm in caregiving. Each situation is unique. We adjust to and meet that uniqueness without being held captive to what the professional literature or even other caregivers present as being standard or benchmark human behavior. They can suggest, but we live the reality. Elaine did just that. She discovered her own unique circle in caring for her mother.

Glimpses of a Daughter and Her Mother

When I try holding on to her arm
As we walk the mall at Ala Moana Center:
"Let go! Let go! You're hurting me!" she yells.
Passers-by stare at the abuser.

She's never one to walk with me.
She's legally blind, you know
So she walks behind me
As we stroll down the mall.

I turn to look behind.
She's turning into Penney's.
Quickly, I touch her arm
To lead her back.

"You're a witch! You're a witch!"
She rants and raves.
In just a second...
Everyone stops to stare
At the abused and the abuser. ✿

More Glimpses of a Daughter and Mother

Down the escalator of Macy's, she stands
Behind me and remarks,
"Your white hair is sticking out!"

This from my mother
Diagnosed legally blind by her physician.

Walking behind me along the aisle of Costco,
She suddenly squeezes my side at the waist
And snaps, "What's this?"
Then her hand grabs the other side.
She remarks loudly, "They're on both sides!"
The Sprint agent roars with laughter.
But I'm not laughing ...

The Handi-Van arrives for her usual pick-up.
"C'mon, Mom, your bus is here."
"Let it wait," she retorts. And she slowly sits down.
Finally, my husband tells her to hurry up
And not to keep the driver waiting, his voice, a bit
gruff.
She turns to walk toward the door and mutters to
him,
"I'll deal with you when I come back!"

Is she the mom who nurtured me?
Is it the dementia playing havoc with my mind?
Or is this really my mom? I don't know. 🌸

In this poem, the message is clear that our loved ones are quite aware of the self that is slowly disappearing. They find creative and resourceful ways to retain whatever human dignity still exists. Listen to Elaine's mother's inner

voice: "Don't question me, what I see, think and hear may
not be in your normal range of senses but they are in mine.
This is all I have and please respect this." Elaine's last
line reminds us how humor sometimes makes all things
tolerable.

The Girl Did It!

"The girl did it!
She made the *shi-shi* and the doo-doo."
My mom utters in a tone of admonishment.

"What girl? Where is she?
What are you talking about?" I question.
"Well, I didn't do this, you spiteful you," she answers.
"Who is this girl?" I ask again,
My frustration and impatience wide open.
"Well, if you don't know, I'm not telling you!"

I pull off the sheets and pillowcase and take them
To the laundry room along with her flannel
nightgown,
Undergarments, and other clothing.

How can she refer to the girl when she observes
Me during the process of cleaning up?

The washer is set, the cycle is complete,
I go to empty its contents only to discover

That the plastic-lined sheeting under her sheets
Are shredded, the cotton batting dissolved
Into very fine threads of yuck.
Such lint you never saw!

I sit down for a few moments to shed some tears.
Then a deep breath...
What else can go wrong? The start of another new
day...
Wash... re-wash... wash again... dry... re-dry...

I'd like to find the girl who did it! 🦑

*In the following episodes, Elaine captures with poignancy
the disease's effect on her mother. Her mother's anger
and even laughter conceal her attempt to cling to her
disappearing self. Elaine's mother reminds us, "Don't ask
me why. I would tell you if I could."*

A Reflection

She folded plastic bags into 2x2's
All creased meticulously, carefully stored
Between books, into handbags,
Stuffed into crevices, nooks, corners.
I ask her why.
"I can't remember," she utters.

She used rubber bands of all colors,
From the Advertiser, Star Bulletin, to carefully

Band sets of five envelopes,
Found in every room of her tiny home.
Some rubber bands, placed on counters and shelves,
"To keep the ants away," she says.

I ask her why.
"I don't remember," she says.

Then there was the money,
Crisp greens of ones, fives, tens, and even twenties
Found between pages, between books,
Inside articles of clothing, in dresser drawers.
I ask her why.
"How do I know?" she retorts angrily.

But the worst, fifteen cylindrical containers of Quaker
oatmeal
All purchased on sale from Longs Drugs or Foodland
Market,
Found in one bedroom all on the floor.
On each lid, little worm-like creatures crawled freely!
"Why so many?" I ask.
She laughs.

Then there are the days she spent
Rummaging through her dresser drawers.
"What are you looking for?" I ask.
She answers angrily,

"I'm looking for... I'm looking for...
I'm looking for something!
Go away!" she answers angrily. ❧

*As the disease worsens, Elaine and her mother appear
to be working out a type of shorthand for communicating
in the days to come. How can so much understanding,
wisdom, awareness, humor, and frustration with what's
happening be contained in a simple word "Humph?"*

*Elaine seems more willing to accept her mother's behavior
without question. What may appear bizarre is quite normal
in the minds of our loved ones. Perhaps if we learn to see
through their eyes and hear through their ears, we will
learn more of their world instead of being stuck in our
own. In turn, we may find a way to live in peace with less
conflict between caregiver and loved one.*

Humph, I Say

I stand at the sink washing the morning dishes
When suddenly I feel a slight whizz on the side of my
neck,
From 5 yards away, the aim is perfect from my
mother.
This was the daily pill as prescribed by her doctor
To curb her feisty behavior.
She has been declared legally blind by her
ophthalmologist!
Humph, I say.

Then there's the protective wear for incontinence.
How often she's refused its usage, a barrage of
denials,
No matter how many times I explain its need.
Found her soiled underclothing in the recesses of her
closet
Or placed between articles of clothing in her dresser
drawers.
She accuses me of entering her privacy.
Her internist says there's nothing wrong.
Humph, I respond.

Then there's the night she woke up screaming.
She shouted about that girl and that man in bed with
her.
"Where's the man?" I stammer.
"Next to me, Can't you see?"
"And where's the girl?"
"Can't you see? Against the wall!"
"Well," I say, "Let the man sleep against the wall.
And put the girl next to you."
"Oh, okay," she utters.
Back to bed I go.
Humph! Humph!

She tells me her false teeth are missing; she can't
find them.
We conduct a search of bathroom and bedroom,
Closets and drawers; look above, under and in-

between
After an hour or so, exhausted and spent
I lay on the floor and, staring at me from under the
dresser
Is her plastic bag of curlers with her teeth.
Are they smiling?
Humph, I cry! ❧

Change is the constant which dogs the caregiver. It strikes by surprise. Elaine's role as caregiver came to her unannounced one night through a simple phone call that drastically changed her lifestyle.

Many caregivers know all too well the one phone call that changes everything. My own call came at a time in my life when I was completely involved with my writing and after-retirement life. The last things I wanted to deal with were family matters and personal responsibilities which I had been happily avoiding like the plague.

I designed my life to be free, but it was not to be when my mother was found wandering in her neighborhood, unable to find her way home. Elaine's next poem also reflects how caregiving closes so many doors and soon isolates us from the art, literature, and music and all that were once regular parts of our lives. Elaine sensed this after the first phone call.

Change

Where did it come from?

    It began with one phone call

    At 9:45 p.m., June 27, 2001

    From Mom who identified herself

    As Natsuyo, instead of Mom.

    She had fallen, taken two hours

    To crawl from the foot of her bed

    To the nightstand for the telephone.

    A rush to her home,

    I find her in her bedroom,

    Lights on.

    A call to 911,

    ER until the wee hours of the morn.

    Finally to a vacant lot

    Where I back my car into a pole.

    Where did it come from?

    This pole in a vacant lot?

Yes, where did it come from?

    My lifestyle of art lessons,

    Movies, restaurants,

    Docent at the Japanese Cultural Center...

    Immediately changed

    With one phone call

    From Mom who called herself

    Natsuyo.

Elaine sent the following note a day after her mother's death:

> When she was under hospice care, her limbs and
> fingernails began to turn grayish as her time was
> approaching. An hour or so after she passed, the gray
> hues left, her nails became the original white, and
> her arthritic right hand became flexible. That was
> so remarkable and I knew then, she was at peace.
> Every so often, I do feel nostalgic and wished I had
> been kinder and more patient during her Alzheimer's
> stage. Life goes on.
>
> Elaine Okazaki
> Honolulu, Hawai'i

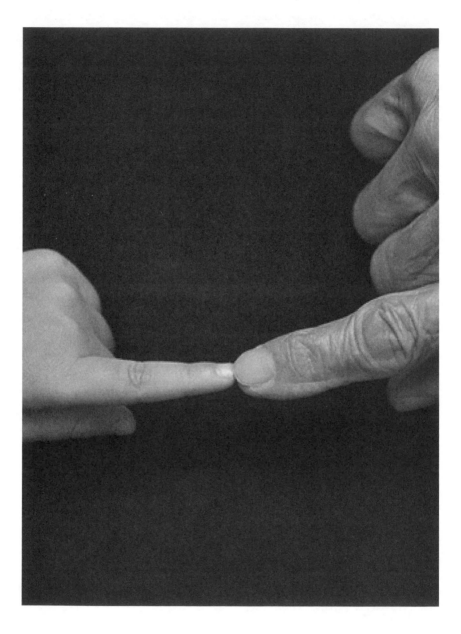

Jason Y. Kimura

Caregiver for his mother:
Lillian Toshie Kimura
(1923 – 2001)

Less than a month ago, Jason listened to me lamenting about "poor me, I'm getting old," and said, "In my eyes, you will always remain that age you were when I first met you." Yes, I like Jason.

He came to my apartment to interview me for a story about my poetry on caregiving and the writing support group I was about to begin for the Alzheimer's Association in Honolulu. My mother sat quietly in the living room working on her row after row of double crochet stitches while Jason and I sat at the dining room table. She turned her head occasionally to check if I were still there.

It was a long interview. I managed to interview Jason, too. I discovered he is a writer and artist. He preserves special moments in his composition notebooks with drawings and words, written late at night after his work-related deadlines are met.

We didn't know then that someday Jason would join my support group as a caregiver. His artistic use of language became an inspiration for our own journal writings. Here, Jason offers excerpts from his journal during the last few days of his mother's life. The entire journal is available through Jason at his email address: jkimura256@gmail. com.

May 9
Mom & Me

And so it finally begins: my mother's descent to her final day. It happened on March 10, my mother's stroke. It was unexpected only from a narrow viewpoint. The week before it happened, she received oxygen in her home. We didn't expect the stroke, but her decline was becoming too obvious not to notice. The stroke was an unforeseen detail in her general descent.

But there can be no complaint concerning my mother. When I was a child, we were very close, but there was always a cloud: my mother had just one lung, less than one, actually, due to tuberculosis in the late 1940s. There was no cure then, except surgery, and to wait in the sanitarium at Leahi Hospital, where, in all, she spent seven years. Not yet married to my mother, my father waited for her against hope. They removed the lung tissue; her teeth rotted away. When she was close to death, they had a cure. They gave the medication to her only for comfort, thinking she was too far gone, but it made her well. My parents were married in 1955, and I was born in 1961. Life for them must have been so fragile, precious, but tenuous, like a silk thread.

Even as a child, I recognized my mother's physical weakness. I was always reticent to leave her side, even for an evening, lest she not be there when I returned. Even at the beginning of my teen years, my heart would tug, ache when we were separated for too long. Much later, when we spoke of her condition, she revealed that the doctors had told her what her life expectancy was. She would never tell me what it was, but

I knew it was short. (My father recently revealed the dread age to be 65.) At 77, it is long past. For that I am grateful.

June 17, Father's Day

We had just reached The Queen's Medical Center's lobby. Jonathan and Jenny (the kids), my wife Kathy and I, half way back to the car, almost free from the burdens of the day, when we heard "Code 500, room 956"over the intercom—my mother's room. I raced back to the elevators while Kathy took charge of the kids. By the time I reached the room, some twenty-odd people—doctors, interns, nurses, hospital chaplain, security officer—had assembled at the room, spilling out into the hallway.

I claimed a floor tile just inside the doorway trying not to take up too much space and peered anxiously at my mother, who minutes before had stopped breathing. In the preceding weeks and months, the anxiety had been coming in waves like nausea, each time the phone rings, the pager beeps, a voice on the other end of the line explains a new development. Today during the crisis, the anxiety was mostly at bay, replaced by numbness, or perhaps exhaustion, physical, emotional, and spiritual.

There has been a crisis every week. Last week it was sifting through Medicare issues for my parents. The week before that, my mother's heart rate went up to 150 and soul-gutting decisions had to be made on her do-not-resuscitate status. The week before that, she had her tracheotomy put in. The week before that, we asked her if she wanted us to remove the ventilator and let her die (which she refused) because we knew it was never going to come off.

The week before that, she was intubated and put on the ventilator after going into respiratory distress. The week before that, I replaced her internist so she could come to Queen's, where I work, and shortly after was brought to the Queen's ER and admitted for rectal bleeding. The week before that, she was rushed to the Kuakini Medical Center's ER because she could barely breathe. The week before that, she came home from her first hospital stay at Kuakini—a fifty-day stay—and Kathy, my father, and I spent eleven hours going back and forth to the pharmacy and other stores for medications and supplies and getting everything in order. The week before that, I went to the hospital on my 40th birthday to learn from therapists how to be a caregiver.

The week before that, there were conferences with social workers and doctors on my mother's prognosis. The week before that, I heard my mother say for the first time that she wanted to die. The week before that, I had to replace unhelpful hospital personnel. The week before that, my mother was in the progressive care unit, struggling to get off the ventilator and finally being freed, while we consulted with the family attorney about unhappy choices. The week before that, she was in the intensive care unit and we didn't know what her prognosis was. And finally, the week before that, I had rushed to ER to find her twitching on a gurney, ventilator tube rudely taped down over her mouth and around her head, and a doctor telling me my mother had a serious hemorrhagic stroke, and that this was probably the end.

The latest crisis was resolved, and the Code Team left one by one. What will next week's crisis be? What will I do when this is all over?

Tuesday, July 3

I sit with my mother and pretend I am 20 years old and that we have as many good years ahead as behind, that her hospital stay is simply a temporary setback, that the three of us—mom, dad, and son—will go on living as we always have. I pretend that this time of togetherness is not temporary like the iridescent colors of a soap bubble, but as permanent as a happy ending forever preserved on celluloid, to be replayed time and again. I wipe saliva from the side of her mouth as casually as I would remove a speck of dust from her blouse. I ignore the ventilator tubes because she sees them not. Instead, I take her hand and hold it reassuringly, pretending not to notice its shaky unsteadiness. She slips her hand out from under mine and puts it on top reassuringly. Perhaps I am no longer 20, but 15, or maybe 10. Either way, I can pretend.

My father called that afternoon to report that my mother had a lot of rectal bleeding. She was though, he said, very awake and responsive. He asked her if she was happy. She nodded affirmatively. Yes, of course I would go to see her later as usual. It seemed just another medical incident to me—one of many that had been occurring on a regular basis. I worked. I worked a bit more, but intended to break in the middle so seeing her would not be the last late event of the day before heading home. I took a break and procrastinated.

At about 4:15 pm, my mother's nurse paged me. Her vitals were failing (or did she say destabilizing?) I should come soon. Was she going to die soon? It was hard to tell from the way the nurse said it. There was no urgency in her voice, but I called my father and told him to come. Somehow, nothing seemed to register. It didn't seem like it would be my mother's last day. There was a deep-seated sense of doom, but there was also a shuddering groan within me, like the great beams of timber in the keel of a ship being pummeled by a stormy sea, and the two emotions co-mingled so as to be indistinguishable. I went to the bathroom to relieve myself, to eliminate what weakness I could, and trotted quickly down the halls.

I got to the room at 4:30. My mother was already gone. Her heart has stopped beating, the nurse informed me. The room seemed airless, as in a vacuum. A single tear rolled down my cheek. I took her hand, but could barely hold it, for it was already as cold as death. The ventilator, which had artificially extended my mother's life, still breathed for her, oblivious of the death of its patient, and continued to part her lips with puffs of air at regular intervals. I was mortified at the icy hand and the heedless ventilator. The nurse explained that she was not allowed to turn it off until my mother was pronounced dead by a doctor, who eventually came in to call the time of death at 4:25—five minutes before I had arrived.

Somehow, although we were adrift at sea, my father and I had made it to shore, as I knew we would. And what does one do, who has been adrift for so long, except to crumble on the wet sand like a once sharp-shiny seashell, tumbled and dulled by the surf, thinking nothing of tragedy or loss—in fact thinking of nothing at all—except for the answer to the question of why God did not take her sooner. Each day of her slow descent had been given to my father, who loved her best, so he could, in his own time, let her go.

Saturday, November 3

I am at the edge of getting past
my mother's long illness,
to see her as she was
in all the years she was well;
but even then,
they are only glimpses.

Jason Y. Kimura
Kailua, Hawai'i

Linda McCall Nagata

Caregiver for her mother:
Geraldine Mary McCall
(1916 – 1991)

Linda was the first post-caregiver to attend my support group. She added a new dimension to grieving after the death of a loved one. Linda came to the group saying, "My mother died twelve years ago and I am still stuck in my grief. I hope this writing support group will help me."

Holidays were bad times for her. She passed greeting card displays in May and felt pain that she couldn't purchase a card for her mother. She dreaded birthdays and the date of her mother's death.

Linda wrote and wept as she shared her work. At the end of the sessions, as other caregivers returned to their loved ones, Linda, too, walked out with the same bundle of daily burdens on her shoulders. After twelve years of silence, all the joy, grief, and intricate details she had blocked from her memories began to surface in her writing.

Unlike the five-stage process of grieving, Linda had her own time line for this process. I am reminded of how I continue to think of my own mother more than eight years after her death. The effects of caregiving and the loss of a loved one continue for a lifetime, and writing helps us to smooth some of the jagged edges.

After exploring those layers of old wounds, the pain and ache buried in them, Linda was the first to leave the group, saying, "I'm ready to move on." She sent me the following letter after leaving us with a batch of poems:

Dear Sensei Frances,

It is true that your encouragement with the writing forced me to look at past events. This is the first year my mother's heaven date was not a time of depression for me. I even got through Valentine's Day and Mother's Day without so much as a tear at the sight of holiday cards in the stores.

Your group and time have softened the previously stone-hard grief in my heart. The grief never goes away, it just gets softer. Thank you for this gift, also.

Thank you for all the help and friendship you have provided. I hope you will continue the group for a long time so others will receive the benefits of writing their stories. You provide a wonderful, loving service to those of us in despair, truly leading us out of our funks.

Love,

Linda

Linda's first poem describes how certain group leaders work in tyrannical mode. She captured my purpose well.

Sensei (Teacher)

She came notebook and pen in hand
To lead me out of my morose state,
Encouraging, cajoling, insisting
Write, write, write.
Others spoke of current dilemmas, emotions.
I was stuck in the past—a dozen years gone by.
"Why am I so emotionally delayed?" my mind asked.
Then the wiser voice said, learn and move on.
Sensei says write, write, write,
Write about one small thing.
I try to focus on one small thing
Dredging up the aged memories
Like buried garbage they are not pleasant,
Helplessness, anger, resentment.
Write, write, write
A miracle happens
The bitter emotions, softened, turn
Into acceptance and peace.
Write, write, write. ✐

*In Linda's second poem, her memory is evoked by ordinary
items like an ornament and sewing tools. Imagine how
after a dozen years or more, the emotions and images are
so clearly seen and so strongly felt.*

Decoration

A small round gold frame
Surfaces in the Christmas decorations
Tiny cross-stitches of red form a G
Intertwined cross-stitches of green form Mc
SMACK, I'm hit again with memories.

Sewing
Next to blood and love
Sewing is our common bond
The planning and construction process
I remember the hours we spent
Looking at patterns and choosing fabrics.
Though miles apart, we chose the same patterns.
Sending sample fabrics back and forth,
You preferring the bold florals,
Me, the calicos.
Now I use your notions when I sew.
I review your patterns,
I feel your presence watching me
Sharing with me the pleasure of creating.
This ongoing bond, it comforts me. ✿

Alzheimer's disease is as slippery as they come, still evasive in medical science.

Covert Activities

Illnesses have turned me into a sleuth.

A self-appointed detective.

With agenda in hand, and without your consent

I write letters to your doctors.

I call your doctors.

Ask questions. Get information.

Research additional information.

Heart attacks, by-pass surgeries, and cancer lend themselves

To this scientific attack. I can deal with those.

There are things to do.

A plan to follow, and always hope for a cure.

Alzheimer's leaves me tilting at windmills.

Nothing to be done.

No plan to follow.

No hope. No cure.

I am powerless.

I turn in my badge.

Even for poets, there are often no words to describe our feelings. Here, Linda uses boxes of chocolate-covered macadamia nuts to express herself to another member of her family.

Chocolates for Doris

Boxes of chocolate-covered Mac nuts.
So simple a gift. My silent way to tell my Aunt
I love her. Words she no longer comprehends.
    She stands in the hall
    Peering at me through clouded eyes
    Like a deer caught in headlights,
    Or a child caught doing mischief.
    She is a wisp of a thing,
    Little of her former robust self remains.
    I take her in my arms
    Hugging a rag doll.
Each box reminds me of the person she was.
Her wonderful story-telling skills,
A lightning quick sense of humor,
The cakes, jams and preserves lovingly made,
Family parties she hosted
With acceptance and love.
I mourn the losses to come
As yet another of my family
Disappears into the dark tunnel.
I want to cling to her

Weeping and wailing like a young child
As Alzheimer's steals her away.
Instead, I offer boxes of chocolates. ❧

Again, there is no blueprint for dying. Things happen, often leaving us with bitter after tastes. My own images of holding my mother's hand as she took her last breath became just that, images. When the head nurse said her pressure was lowering, I didn't know in medical terms that she was dying. I left, intending to return in the afternoon. She drew her last breath soon after I left her room. In "Death," Linda voices her own questions about her mother's last moment.

Death

There is no death with dignity for you.
My strong, silent mother.
You who had always been Miss Manners, kind and
thoughtful.
Instead death comes on a dark winter night
When you are alone—hospitalized.
The cancerous tumor bursts.
You cough rivers of blood.
Until all life has been expelled.
Violent death, with no dignity for an ever-gentle soul.

There is no right time or best time for caregiving. There is also no preparation for this daunting task except for long-term-care insurance, trusts, and wills. Linda uses the metaphor of a sandwich to explain how she, a full-time working parent, found herself in the middle of two slices of bread that often choke and paralyze the filling in the center.

The Sandwich

I'm in the middle
Caught between an increasingly forgetful mother
And a rebellious daughter.
Mom can't remember short-term things
She says inappropriate things
Acts in inappropriate ways
Dresses inappropriately
Happy one instant, crying the next.
Daughter is demanding and self-centered
Starts down the path of alcohol and drugs
Temper tantrums worthy of a two year old
I am torn between two needy factions.
Mom unaware, daughter pushing all boundaries
Both out of control.
My strength seeps out.
The sound of my daughter's demanding voice,
Mom, crying and not understanding what is
happening,
I am being pushed to the edge.
Is there anyone to help me? ✀

This next poem goes to the source of many of the heartaches that beset caregiving: Family. The word family connotes wholeness, oneness, connectedness and loving support, an ideal bound to conflict with the desires of individuals. A family consists of individuals and their own personal set of values, life situations, and their own relationships. To expect equal participation, interest, or support from each member of the family may not be a reality.

Caregiving is long term, and each member's value system may not fit into caregiving for aging parents. To have family members rise to the occasion of caregiving full-heartedly is often a rarity. I have seen so many families disintegrate as they end in attorney offices, bickering over finances, living wills, and trusts and voicing complete distrust of family members.

It seems that, whether functional or dysfunctional, family structures have already been established long before a family member comes to need caregiving. These fragments often remain long after caregiving.

Resentment

I was full of resentment.
Life was anchored in resentments.
Resentments ate away at me
Fueling my unhappiness and rage.
Why was I expected to "take care of " everything?
Didn't others see they could help?
Why did others ask what they could do to help, and not follow through?
My resentments built, one incident after another.

I felt entitled to hold these resentments
Take them out and mull them over, and over, and
over
See what a good person I am, I do everything
Others set me up and expect me to "take care of"
I set myself up and expect myself to "take care of."
Later I learned I couldn't control other people, places
or things.
I can only do what I can do for myself
Expecting my family to help allows them to have
power over me.
How freeing to have learned this lesson. ❧

Linda writes:

> It has now been 15 years since my Mom's death. In
> that time, my father has died, also my favorite Aunt,
> and many friends. I have seen the resentments in
> others tasked with being caregivers; been brought to
> tears at unexpected memories of a departed friend;
> become a grandmother placing the rebellious daugh-
> ter in the "sandwich" position; and experienced the
> ongoing peaks and valleys of emotions that make life
> a tapestry.
>
> It's been a "hell of a ride," and I'm looking forward to
> MORE! Which way to the roller coaster?
>
> Linda McCall Nagata
> Kaneohe, Hawai'i

Red Slider

Caregiver for his mother:
Isobel
(1919 – 2005)

Once upon a time in Sacramento, a caregiver named
Red Slider dragged himself to his computer to Google
"Caregiving/Poetry." For almost ten years he'd been caring
for his mother Isobel, who had Alzheimer's disease. Before
that he was passionately committed to writing poetry. He
was curious to see if anyone was also writing poems about
caregiving. At that time, only one item appeared, the title of
my book, Mosaic Moon. He ordered the book, liked what he
read, and wrote to the publisher, who forwarded his email
to me. He attached a poem called "Without Appointment"
that was inspired by one of my poems.

It was unlike any other fan mail I had received. His
thoughts set his letter apart: "I tell myself there is no time,
but in reality, there are no words. Perhaps later, when
it is all over, there will be time. I'm not sure there will
be words." His emails and poems were shared with my
second support group in Honolulu and he was considered
an Internet member.

Stories and even introductions that begin with "Once upon
a time" are expected to end happily ever after, and this
introduction is no different. I was invited to Seattle and
Sacramento to speak at a conference and at adult day

care centers and dropped by to see Red since I was in the neighborhood.

Not long after, 51 boxes of my belongings and I arrived at his front door, which was left wide open. I was left standing in the living room amongst my baggage while Red disappeared to attend to Isobel. We both cared for his mother Isobel until her death.

Red's first poem, "Without Appointment," is presented with a journal entry that takes us on a bewildering journey in a world often short on understanding.

It was an appointment at a clinic that began my journey with Isobel into the dark side of life's fragilities. It was on that day that I first understood the puzzling scruff marks on the top of her shoe as we climbed the clinic steps and her dragging toe scraped over each tread. Little did I know then what terrible burdens were hidden in such a simple task as keeping an appointment. For the next fifteen years I would sadly come to learn the horror of the word, "appointment". But on that particular day (the first occasion on which I had ever accompanied Isobel on a visit to her doctor), it was just another appointment to see what was taking so long about diagnosing and treating some vague problem with her right foot and leg.

After that, there were inexorable waits as I followed along from diagnosis to diagnosis. What started as "drop-foot" progressed to "shin splint" and then to "pinched nerve" and onward and upward as "carpal-tunnel syndrome" until I finally could no longer sit idle and watch her "managed care" degenerate into "mangled care."

That was the beginning of our strange journey down this rabbit hole of medical appointments. Alzheimer's wasn't even a word in our vocabulary at that time. It would be another year before we'd turn to that page in the dictionary. But the word "appointment" was, and its meaning loomed ahead of us in ways we could never have imagined. It was on that day of our first unsteady climb up the clinic stairs that I mark as the day, unbeknownst to either of us, I signed on as Isobel's caregiver. How could I have known then that I'd made an appointment that could not be canceled?

Without Appointment

There was no announcement
hardly a sound, a foot-scruff
on the steps to the clinic,
a slow walk, more delay
and no surprises.
Neither broadside nor listings
give date or time, fashionably late
for the spoon to drop
to the floor with a loud
Clang like a tin gong.
A door flung open
to a morning of strange sentences
mushed into vacant syllables
Da-da abbing, abba dobbing
over their own cadence.
Nothing is circled
on this calendar;

not the day her knees buckled,
the wild sounds in moan
or bone beat on thunder drum.
No one was on hand to introduce
the slump thing in the wheelchair,
with an RSVP that was never sent.
Forgive us for barging in this way.
Forgive us for being late, as usual.
Forgive us our sudden intrusion,
our insubordination, our guileless moon.
There, where there is matted grass,
our bewildered bare feet went.

Red's next poem speaks of the irony of Isobel, a former Reading Specialist, struggling with the very skills that supported her lifetime career and passion.

The Reading Specialist

Pulling down the window shade
of page, pink emery board pressed
beneath her fingers, she reveals
each line, each line unraveled,
each undeciphered word, pure sound,
ripples of phoneme without meaning
that crackle on the dry parchment.
"It's from, I think it's from, my daughter,"
she says. She says, "She's having a baby.
They'll come and show me, maybe tomorrow."

But the secret of that spring,
so many springs ago, is caught in the crease
on the blue page with the little yellow flowers,
worn through from too many years of renewal.
Desperately, she tries to refold the torn
halves of faded event. Too late.
The sounds spill their vacant contents
onto the floor.
For a moment, recognition catches
in her throat. Then, voiceless,
the parchment shudders,... erasing. ❧

*The title of the next poem hints at a double layer of
happenings. Red describes in detail the preparation of an
egg, the tiny fractures in its smooth shell, and the tearing
of the membrane. But, is it only the egg's membrane that is
being torn and fractured?*

Redoubled

The eyes were large and moist,
following every move with
intense interest, (each fragment)
of egg folding over the edge
of the cup as the shell withdrew,
moistening the rose medallions,
lifting a petal in bold relief
above the dull gloss of porcelain
sky oozing onto the table.

Wrinkled fingers, pale, delicate,
fold over themselves,
strain against smooth surfaces.
Bright red nails probe the taut
immobility of time, seek imperfection,
tiny fractures in implacable shell;
(mother, would you like them poached?)
muffled sounds of thin membrane... tearing. ❧

*Listen to the befuddled voice of Isobel. Is she speaking to a
friend she no longer recognizes, or is she simply conversing
with herself? The last line tells us how she is absolutely
sure/unsure. Another prominent trait of the disease:
there is no way to assess reality as one's measuring stick
eventually disappears.*

Revisitation

Come in, my dear, if you must;
it was inevitable that we meet this way,
was it not? You look so well and I,
but no matter if we are strangers
meeting like this face to face,
we have met before, on the steps
to reach this place, have we not?
Of course we have, though
I've never seen you before, have I?
Still, we are together, you and I,
All our lives we circle one another,

exchanging small favors along the way,
Do we not? Do we not? Of course
we don't! I've never seen you before.
I'm quite sure. Yes, now I'm quite sure. ∂♫

*Caregivers often express, more than once, how writing
helps to release all the rage, frustrations, sorrow, and
helplessness of caregiving. Not to be ignored, also, is the
salvation found in humor that stops us from becoming a
total casualty.*

Untitled

Only ritual marks the day
in the days that have lost
all trace of beginning or end
in this night without end.
Each day I keep my watch,
by night I sift through ashes,
"Surely, somewhere in all of this
must be the hand of God?"

Caregiver: "I sifted through the ashes today and,
indeed
found that the hand of God was in there, after all."
Social Worker: "And what did you do then?"
Caregiver: "Handed Him a subpoena
for a product liability lawsuit." ∂♫

*Nightbook #1 offers a powerful magnifying glass to follow
Red, during one night of caring for Isobel, allowing us
an intricate and jolting look at all the events, past and
present, thoughts and observations that happen or don't
happen, in a minute-by-minute account, taking us into the
running thoughts of the caregiver as the minutes tick away
into another unending day.*

NIGHTBOOK #1:

Half-past three, in camera: I awake and lay on the mat,
checking the vague need I had to pee. Checking the tense.
Not sufficient to normally arouse me, but I decide I will try
anyway. So I roll off the mat and go to the next room and
relieve myself in the dark. Just as I thought, not enough
to bother. But my sense of "bother" is no longer mine. The
return to the bedroom is blazed with unfocused eyes, regis-
tered in a slightly darker shadow over the pitch of the living
room. Something there is less visible than the fabric of dark-
ness. "Mom?" I check my question. The barely discernible
shape is perceptibly denser against the regular lines of the
sofa. Doesn't move. Should it? I check my senses. Her hand
in mine, I can now unwrap her from the heavy Indian knit
blanket with the other, taking care not to squeeze anything
at all as she no longer tolerates even the slightest intrusion,
the least ambient pressure. It is all that is left of her defense
system—the gentlest touch, a potential killing blow.

Half-past-three-with-searchlight: Even so, she warns from
somewhere in the lightless muddle, "Don't hurt me!" I check
my defenses. "Mom, I'd never hurt you." But I know I do, a

hundred times every day. Pouring her hand into the sleeve of her robe, patting her on the shoulder after pushing the chair up to the table, a sock-snag on a toenail (and when, I wince, should I treat her to the agony of cutting them?). A simple difference, the gradient a couple of molecules make scurrying one way or the other over open skin registers like a shard of ice drilled through her chest, my fingers just grazing her throat throws her head back against the chair, the last button on her blouse is lost and I will have to start over.

Half-past-three-oh-one: Mom? What are you doing sitting here? A rhetorical question: a probe for a phrase of bewilderment. More often, now, just the guest whimper of consciousness. I make approach noises, intone the prowl of bears at the margins of a campsite to have her stand up. She answers with a short moan, a faint foghorn signal in muddle so thick one cannot even see the mental images inside one's own mind.

Awake and lost, I think to myself, log it. I press the "jungle-Jim" of my forearm against her as familiar prehensile reflexes take over. Frail hands grasp the bar of my arm. Pull yourself up, Pull! We do "The Lift" together, ignoring everything but the exact forces needed to slowly raise her to her feet. Too little grasp or too much pull by fractions of an ounce and we'll lose it and have to start over. It is a successful maneuver this time as I slip my arm around her waist like a safety bar and walk her back up the hall toward her bedroom.

Three-twenty-seven at half-past-three-oh-two: What I don't know is whether she got lost before or after the hall outside the bathroom directly across from her bedroom. And if she

got to the bathroom, did she recognize the toilet? And if she
recognized it, did she know what to do? And if she did, did
she even remember what she got up to go there and do in
the first place? Probably not. I do a quick check of the toilet
as we reach that end of the hall, synched in what I call her
"Chinese steps." A small piece of tissue with other evidence
of use. The tissue from before? I can't recall. Mom, do you
have to peepee?

The juvenilia come easy. At first they masked the breach of
realms: personal function with diminutive innocence. Then
it covered the recognition of breach with immediate distrac-
tions, silly humor and sounds regressive. Finally, a natural
vocabulary that is all that is left of recognition. Clinical
terms don't register at all anymore; normal usage sets off
a panic of trying to recall meanings that refuse to identify
themselves. "Pee-pee" and "poop" it is.

Half-past-three on three-fifty: After that, I don't know, we're
not quite there yet. Sometimes, it's just plain instinct. I have
kids somewhere, she might say. Her hand moves uncertainly,
I check tenses, across her chest, down her hips, as she pulls
at her pant legs. Oh, you need to pee? (I know how I knew
what that meant the second time, but how did I know how to
translate that the first time?) You're talking too fast, I don't
understand. I adjust the pace by half-a-minute: You need to
pee-pee? Maybe, toilet? Pee-pee? Oh, yes, I think so. Soon the
whole matter (by instinct) will be managed by instinct alone.
For now I'm just thankful that she can hold her crotch and
look around for something she should be doing. Thankful for
that, and Depends.

An-hour-past-three: It is done. We make it to the bed without further excursion. I pull the warmth of the electric blanket over her. I will need to get her up early and take her to "school." The installation of the new heat pump will require inside duct work as well. It is not her regular daycare day but the confusion would disturb great swatches of molecules, diffuse them into the noise of passing workmen, hoist them from cranes lowering three-and-a-half tons of cube onto the roof, smear them under boots over sagging rafters. It is enough to watch minute amounts of her leak out into the vapor of rattling breakfast dishes and the sequence of steps from first light to first shoe, gone forever into the vacuum of life.

She enjoys watching the million dollar quiz. Right or wrong, the questions and answers are a continuous stream of nonsense. The money is nonsense. But the refusal to answer a question, the confession of emptiness, that she understands. She cheers the confessor. She is satisfied to see them handed a check for not having an answer. She asks how she can get on that program.

Half-past-three-oh-five: My acquired-mother antennae do a bed-check in the dim light. I will need to stay for awhile until she is drifting. Otherwise, she will be up again in ten or fifteen minutes.

Loneliness was driving her tonight. It doesn't go away, it merely is overcome. I rest my hand lightly on her shoulder and we fall into a regular breathing pattern—I suppress my own consumptive hacking. It works. Five minutes later I get up and go back to bed.

Half-past-three, en molé: I laugh as I roll onto the hard
mats between bouts of wheezing, apnea, hacking and decid-
ing whether to peel my socks off my gout-bloated shins
and expose them to the relief of the arctic temperatures in
my room. Hell, I'm sicker than she is. Sicker, poorer, cra-
zier, more forgetful (what does she have to remember?),
depressed, lonely, numb, depersonalized and flat out burned
out. I laugh again. Grief? Ah yes, the thing that's stuck
somewhere between "laugh" and "laugh."

My friend's words, the ones he sent me after burying his
father, run through my head as I roll on my back and wait
for the day's nicotine toxemia to settle down. He talked about
the "grail of pain" and I think, There isn't a one of us in the
bunch—friends, wives or passers-by—who hasn't asked him
for a prescription at one time or another. I turn over and get
up. Nightbook waits in the workroom like a dense shadow.

An hour-ago: Days ago: the year when my father died:
Between "laugh" and "laugh" there is "half," "shaft," "graft,"
"craft," "thief," "belief," "relief," and momma shadows in the
living room; and, on the other-side, "reef." "beef," "blown
leaf," "creative," "evasive," "instinctive," "flawed," "chas-
tened," "aging," "full/empty" and half-daft years ago: with a
deep-space vacuum where my father once stood in the way,
"Other" is shaving myself in the mirror; responsible where I
was knee-deep in drifting, hidden where I was exposed, powerful where I could only be clever or, worse, deceitful. But he
is there with the goods and whatever good another mirror
can reveal.

Half-past-ground-zero: Why, "they" ask, do you think your family so thoroughly turned against you? I prattle something about "who owns mom," the stock social worker's answer. Grief? A distraction from listening to what I already know. They scream, chatter like monkeys, throw feces through the cage bars, cheat, withhold support, covet power, make threats and spoil everything else. A composite picture of the "family father"—pater monster—since his death. Am I supposed to ally myself with that image—to offer up my mother to their rendition of him like an almond-eyed china-doll on a lacquered shelf? I laugh now.

In thirty-five years I never spoke to him. But it's they who hate his guts, right down to the last bad bedside fart before he died. I was barred from that opus (it might kill him, one said of the possibility I might visit him in the hospital). But, I still remain the only family who knew anything about his heart—the one that really killed him. It was too big to let out, so he buried it in shit where no one could find it—brutality, threat, work, power, distance, burden and the rest of a smoldering pile of very smelly stuff (he had a body odor that knocked us all out) made it a very difficult object to find.

I knew him like a mirror, though. I was a damned good mirror. Left where he was right, dumb where he was smart, evasive where he was direct, lazy where he was dutiful... I hid all the forms—my brutal honesty, my self-destructive energy, the burden of my mission, my painful brilliance, "see, never dry" creativity (recall he was a writer, too) in forms he'd never suspect, never realize, were just mirror images of himself. He reached for the grail of pain, and couldn't let go, and wouldn't bargain. So he hid it instead. In dung, never noticing the right hand of God was now to his left.

(*check tenses*): He looked in the mirror. I looked back and saw the face of a fully terrorized man, the eidos of pain. What did he see? He saw me cringe with fear, and he was satisfied. Like a sign over buried plutonium, made to last 10,000 years, he had warned me away the only way he knew would work. He loved me, so he terrified me until he was sure I would not go "there." Thanks, pop. And now that I know what you did, I know what to do with it. It's ok, dad, I can take it from here. Let it go now, old man. It got buried in shit but I found it, even if I had to wade, in order to find it. You can rest in peace now.

6am: Soon she will be standing in the kitchen, just off this workroom. She will be completely confused. The lights from here, the dark in there, the table, chairs, a clock, the stove pot will all be strangers. I stop and go to her. She says, "Let's go home now." I am relieved that she still recognizes me. I answer, "Today is a 'school day.'" I'll put on some fresh coffee and Miles Davis and then we'll get you dressed and ready. Oh good, she replies, I want to go to school now.

Nightbook #2, a provocative piece filled with powerful language and images, takes us to the dark side and its shadows, on a journey into the almost endless well of grief. The journey takes us to the eyes, where eventually all human functions retreat, like Dian Fossey's gorillas. In the end, they stare back at us, communicating nothing. Or is this conclusion just an illusion?

Red's selection of the ape metaphor is consistently used to describe the unexpected effects of this disease on a human being. Filled with metaphors—apes and monkeys, onions being peeled to nothing—Red ends his nightbook with resounding hope, for what else is there when synapses connect, disputing scientific and medical research?

NIGHTBOOK #2

Koko ("ko-ko") the clown was a Max Fleischer character from the "Out of the Inkwell" cartoon series. "Out of the Inkwell" was produced from 1918 to 1929.

(Nightbook recalls ko-ko to the stand)

Staving off early releases from the hospital and progressing to Medicare "Bills of Demand" leaves little time (perhaps less enthusiasm) to write. In the middle section of the third stage of Alzheimer's (or seventh, depending on how many fingers the principal investigator had on one hand), the fabric of grammar itself begins to tear as one watches the signifier retreat unexpectedly into eyes which seem to appreciate that the betrayal of the mouth has begun. The signifieds loosed in every direction careen against one another. Many are murdered on the spot; some simply stumble blindly or fall in place spinning uselessly. But the eyes, like the incomparable wells of pathos and curiosity Dian Fossey once recorded from the faces of another species, can do nothing to stem the carnage on the table in front of them.

They stare, they move, they moisten and dilate as one hand leaves fingerprints on the carmelated sweet potatoes and the other drops the spoon gripped loosely in the funnel of a closed fist. Even the large wet question laced across the iris dissolves in its own insufficiency and the fingers give up their clutching at useless stones. They yield to the weight of

a limp hand dragging them through the spaghetti sauce and
onto her lap. I am just recovering the spoon when I look up to
see her eyes like those of some bewildered Kong.

They will say she has progressed and discuss strategies
for feeding and delight over the few remaining indicators
of interest or pain or love that bubble up from time to time
through the corpses of words laying in their little pools of
disaffection. But I have heard the last of her last real words:
"I am dying, I am dying. It's all broken. Bring me things, not
news. I can't choose the blue instabul weel-um stratus imbu-
latus all begumble with me. Let's go."

I am peeled back as her eyes move side-to-side studying my
face as though it were a landscape. I avert my own eyes until
I can stand it no longer. I look at the eyes that look directly
at mine looking at her. I have nothing to say. I drop the
spoon.

The Ink and the Fury

Ink and the fury of a hundred monkeys typing
would not produce a single word remembered
as it would have bloomed, but in this garden
only dark lit sparks drip from thoughts as remote
as the liquid anvil on which the stars are hammered.
In these words I find motion, but around them
how quickly, "I am dying, I am dying," she says.
"Bring me things, not news." Surrounded by the ineffable,
her gorilla eyes say things with desperate appeal
as she retraces her steps backward, in a dementia
uncertain of time, to a place where news only ricochets

and words misfire into thickets of useless confusion;
the night-bloom of inkwells back-filling ahead of her.
Those and a few stray remarks pass through yesterday's
center of an indwelling aphasia filled with permanent ink.
Her Cho-Cho gives it up, resigned to the black sea of
its origin, the upwelling end of all appeals, "Bring me
things," she says. No more, her closed lips pressed to
the side of an empty fist as she signs her desire to eat,
pulling the stopper down tight.

MORNING BREAK:

She's in the other room, feeding herself. You need to realize
this is an accomplishment worthy of an Olympic gold medal.
It begins with lacing a boot or taping a wrist or taking a
warm-up lap or drawing to an inside straight. Six months
ago I was barely able to feed her. A bad reaction to a new
medication lit her up like the sun and dropped her like a
limp rag doll.

Now she can hold a spoon by herself, in signature simian
fashion, and put away her favorite foods with the gusto of an
athlete in training. This was not supposed to be possible, as
Alzheimer's victims cannot learn anything new. The mind
peels itself away like an onion until only the peel and the
whir of the garbage disposal remain. The residue, where
the action ought to be, is simply tangles of plaque and fused
wiring hopelessly burnt to a cinder.

But, she did learn and from God knows what reserve. It
won't last forever, but for now it's impossible not to begin
each morning with the sense there's a torchbearer in the

background clearing the tunnel and igniting the flame. In the distance, there is the daily call: "LET THE GAMES BEGIN."

The Last Olympiad

She tied that bow
with such perfect concentration,
pulling the loop around
the index, saddling the bitter end,
done at last when she'd coaxed
the lace over the arthritic arch
on her bony finger,
and finished the job
with a tug
and a grunt.

A blue sneaker waves a happy foot
in triumph. The flaming arrow of Olympus,
her cane, taut as a bow,
the torchlight shining from her eyes.
I'm ready to go, she says on the final lap
to the door. "Not quite," I say
as I hand her the other shoe
for her grueling decathlon.
Today, a silver medal performance,
tomorrow, who knows, perhaps
her buttons will be done correctly? 🌿

The Day You Became Isobel

Not on the days you lost your keys,
or the words you couldn't quite recall,
or the puzzles unsolved in the Sunday Times.
Not when the refrigerator got lost,
or the steps home untraceable,
or the faces of your children unrecognized.

It was on the day I returned to your name
for the sake of my memory as much as yours.
I said, "Isobel" to remember the you of you,
and whenever I spoke about you to them,
or to myself about you; or called out to you,
"Isobel, it's time for lunch. Isobel, I'm here."
That was the day you became so much more
than the ghost of a changed person,
a "she was" stuck in my native thought;
more than that, so much more than "mom." ❧

And then there is death and dying. My business, my mission of care, was about life. I had no say in defining death. I had everything to say about defining life. When I understood that, and not before, I understood that what we do as caregivers is far larger than simply something we do for ourselves or our loved ones. On more than one occasion Isobel had toed-up to that line that marked the end of the journey.

One time, a bladder infection had taken her to that edge. Septicemia set in and the doctors held little hope for her recovery. "Heroic measures" were out. Palliative care and cessation of all treatment were the other option the doctors offered. "Why?" I asked myself. True, she was elderly and, yes, she had Alzheimer's. But what did that mean? That she was old and not useful and should therefore be left to die?

That was the moment that I understood that only the caregiver stands in the way of such shallow definitions of mortality. I instructed the doctors to continue Isobel's medication and treatment. "No heroics," I said, "Just do what you would for someone half her age and without Alzheimer's. Then let's see what happens." Two weeks later, Isobel recovered. It was from that moment that I began to refer to caregivers as "Stewards of Mortality."

The Caregiver's Reply

There will come a day;
and on that day
beings from beyond the stars
will come to ask,
"Why should the likes of you,
defective and dangerous as you are,
be permitted to spread beyond
the light of your dying sun
and onto the wonder of the heavens?"

In reply, a single caregiver
stepped out from the cloud of humanity
as if to say, "We are the Stewards of Mortality.
In all the limitless expanse of your travel,
the countless species of your wondrous universe,
have you ever met the likes of us?" ✣

One of Isobel's favorite poems was Oliver Wendell Holmes' "The Deacon's Masterpiece" or, "The Wonderful One-Hoss Shay." It was, of course, the model for how she preferred to meet the end of life; not in "the hundred-years-and-a-day," but to leave when the time came, all at once without some prolonged collapse.

That, of course, wasn't to be. But, as much as I could, I kept her engaged in life and "up and running" until it was done. That much I could do. The rest was up to her. It was her schedule and I was determined to let her circle the calendar in whatever fashion suited her, whether it was an appointment at the clinic, or a date with death.

I returned a minute later with a glass of water in my hand and stood in the doorway. I didn't have to go any nearer to know she had chosen that moment to die—all at once, at home, the way she'd wanted.

Still:

> In death, the moonlight,
> Closer than an empty bed,
> An unlit doorway

Red Slider
Sacramento, California

Eugenie Mitchell

Caregiver for her mother:
Joyce J. Mitchell
(1928 -)

When Genie first entered the room where my third writing support group was being held, I mistakenly thought, "She can't be a caregiver, not with such an aura of peace and serenity." I later smiled when she said, "I'm not sure about poetry. I'm too practical, too ploddingly pedantic." Poetry writing seemed far-removed from the writing she had done in her career. Genie gave up her law practice and partnership in Sacramento a few years after becoming a caregiver for her mother about ten years ago.

Her notes to herself read, "Too self-conscious. That's how poetry has always seemed to me. But now being self-conscious is precisely what I want to be because I am afraid I am losing myself, or becoming a self I don't want to be."

Her first poem, called "Stuffing It," opened a floodgate of writing, and she attends each of our monthly sessions bringing a batch of new poems. Genie's journey reminds me of a river. Whatever the currents, turbulent or serene, she takes the river as it flows, with humor, tears, poetic reflection and pragmatism, protecting her mother with vigilance and love.

Genie's first three poems speak of the realities of caregiving. Often a small voice of guilt dwells in caregivers saying, "It's not nice to complain or to speak of the harsh realities of caregiving. How can a good human being complain when the ones being cared for are suffering?" One of the wonders of poetry is that it raises these realities to a higher level of experience and helps caregivers deal openly with the truth of what goes on daily, if not hourly.

Stuffing It

This is what I do.
I stuff it.
I stuff all my emotions
and when the day is done,
I stuff myself
with sugar and fat.

And then there's Mom.
How sweet she is ... usually...
most of the time...
I'm lucky she's sweet;
she's lucky, too.
Lucky?
Neither of us is
Lucky. 🍃

have i given up?

have i given up?
i feel the tightness in my chest

that means anxiety
too much stress
high blood pressure,
heart attack and stroke
or maybe it means my heart is bleeding
metaphorically
for love is not enough
i have not the strength to be sufficient
no matter my intentions
i cannot live her life for her
and i can't live mine with her by my side

i am tired of living her anxiety
as she's talked so much her mouth is dry
she's said it feels all stuck inside
and still talks on and on and on
as she shuffles around the house
lifting every object with shaking hands and
placing it
somewhere more precarious for it
and more perilous for her
as she struggles to pull the cushion up she's sitting on
an activity both violent and funny
as she yanks the power cords from their hiding place
behind the furniture
and lays new traps to trip herself
as i switch on the bathroom light to encourage her
to chat with the lady in the mirror
and her hands keep turning the water on

    dropping the soap dish into the unseen

    depression of the basin

    unrolling lengths of toilet tissue

    as if she were a kitten

as in her latest inability to sit still

    she stumbles to a stand

    pitches two steps forward

    pivots and sits upon me

    oblivious to my limbs

as i try to invent new ways to warn her

    and dissuade her, redirect her but reassure her

    ways that sound calm and pleasant

    not panicked and fed up

i am ashamed to admit

i cannot tolerate another instant

    of drudgery

    of masking my emotions

    of living with this excruciating death

with so much life going on within it

but also passing by

and then i know

how neglect can transpire

i can't stand it

    i have to stand it

i would rather be screaming ❧

Medium Resistance

I contemplate yet another inadequacy.
My predecessor poets became their mothers'
advocates –
as media imagining the healthy thoughts of a brain
diseased
and voicing these imaginings through poetry.
But not me. Not this J.D.

The lazy-crazy-stupid ADD-me
writes about resenting daily drudgeries,
procrastinating these banalities
in a vain attempt to banish them, magically.

Yet, I feel I have surrendered me sufficiently.
I am the wheeled chair for Mom's cognition,
and I am the curator of her life's collections.
I am already my mother's memory.

So I resist residing inside her mind
and disappearing entirely. ৶

The return to childhood behavior brings anxieties and feelings of sorrow as we live with the progressive deterioration of our loved ones. Yet, as Genie poignantly points out, this same behavior was once ironically hers when she was a child, and it was nurtured by her mother.

Society

When I was three or four
we had a sandbox in our yard
where I played
with my friend Jane.
I amused us both
by baking pretend pies
on my little kiddie stove.

When Mommy called me
to our real lunch
I always invited Jane.
Mommy set an extra place
and divvied up the carrot sticks
and sandwiches to share.

Jane was good, and polite - I saw to that,
passing along her every word of praise.
She even returned her uneaten food
so it wouldn't go to waste.
Mommy relished that -
as she cleared the dishes
from Jane's empty place.

So now when Mom summons "everyone"
to accompany us to the store,
or cajoles that "nice lady" in the mirror
to "come, come have fun" with her,

or worries that "all those people" I cannot see
haven't had enough to eat,
I mouth the-more-the-merrier,
not so much to humor Mom,
as to honor her,
for helping me to meet my need for society
when my brain was playing tricks on me
fifty years before. ✷

Genie turns the seemingly simple act of helping her mother dress into a graceful bullfighter's dance while capturing a delightful conversation. I say "seemingly simple" because nothing is simple when one attempts to pull stiffened arms and legs through sleeves and pants.

The Bullfighter

I am the *torero*.

I hold not a cape, but her coat,
    a bright French blue
    instead of Spanish red.

I regard my other.
    Slight and vulnerable,
    she is animated, talking silly and senseless.
    Or, she is silent and absent.

I hold her coat
    off to my left
    for my *paso*
    to her right.

I move the sleeve toward its position.
I follow her restless right arm.
I feint slightly to her left
    drawing her toward me.
Quickly, I reverse,
    pushing the sleeve
    toward her arm again.

Her arm mimics my moves,
    but remains out of reach.
Eluded.
A failed *faena.*
Thus we commence our toreador dance.
    I am following her arm,
    and she is following mine.

Blue cloth outstretched between us,
    we circle and circle
    in our own *pasodoble.*
I am the *torero.*

But I am not the *matador.*
And she is not a bull. ❧

Can This Daughter Be Trusted?

Pull up your pants.

    I don't have any pants.
These are your pants.

    Aren't I a girl?
Yes. Girls can wear pants.

    These pants are too tough.
Tight. I'll help you.

    Don't knock me off.
Sorry. I'm pulling up your pants.

    I thought you were knocking me off.
No, I love you. I'm trying to help you.

    You're killing me.
I'm pulling up your pants.

    I thought I was going to die.
You're not going to die.

(Oops. Her eyes know the lie.) ❧

It takes a caregiver to understand how a simple errand can become a 595-word poem. We all have our Costco stories. Only after caregiving did I became aware of certain people needing help and empathy in public places. Perhaps someday, when post-caregivers are out in numbers, there will be more shoppers who will understand why our loved ones may sometimes throw tantrums in supermarket aisles, tell a stranger he's handsome or beautiful, or talk back to cartoons on cereal boxes. This is a time when embarrassment and suspicion might turn into patient acceptance or even an occasional helping hand.

I Hate Costco

I hate Costco.
Cavernous assault on our senses,
dangerous decibels and fluorescence,
caustic reek of hotdog essence –
gargantuan consumption is its quintessence.

Hefty, beefy families of five,
moon-faces ballooning over
    loads of chips
    and fifty rolls
    of toilet tissue –
the Costco lesson is just this:
excess becomes
excrement.

And yet we take the bait –
    six tens of Depends
    six dollars less,

and here we are,
cart crammed with cartons
lime and pink
in lurid proclamation
of our own excretion.

Next we navigate ironically,
the cleanly row of godly laundry,
stocking up in triplicate,
    Clorox bottles in a box,
    forty-plus pounds
    of rigorous wrangling.
I struggle and sweat, then find success –
    only to lose…
    my mom.

Invisible I
while bent with bleach,
so too did she
disappear from view.
Is she plodding along, trailing only the tide?
Or has a dimpled infant lured her aside?
Maybe she's made for the exit,
    ever unerring destination
    despite her disorientation.

I shout her name down every lane,
disturbing the massive multitudes
into silent aversion,

their meditations transcended
by my intrusion –
but all to no avail.

Afraid to foray
in the parking lot,
and afraid to not,
I teeter at the door
where the checkers listen
to my description
and send a signal
throughout the store.

She is all field-mark,
     as the birders say,
hair white as any bald eagle's pate,
her plumage a coat of sage,
with purple pants
and bells atinkle on her toes.
Though arrayed so vividly,
she is but a little titmouse
among these giant predators.
I fear... No. I check myself.
I had better hope
she is not their prey.

Fighting the blinding red rise
of plain old panic –
Stay calm!

What to do?
Think!
But not of evil!
How could I lose her?
Stupid Clorox!
Bad daughter!
Move! Move!
Do something!
What?

I finally espy her white hair's crest,
bobbing slowly
in the teeming sea of being.
She emerges in pure purple,
green coat a wad in her arms.

The relief of reunion is only mine:
Mom is fine.
For her, there is
nothing not normal:
she never knows her whereabouts.

Now I propel our bounty to purchase,
    clenching her arm to my side,
    pretending to be her escort,
As we resume our unstately, glacial parade
to the checkstand, our last resort.

The line is long, Mom is tired.
She does not understand the line idea.
She loudly proclaims
that she does not know my name,
and why should she do what I say?
The multitudes no longer look away.

Antsy in the crush at the door,
    Mom feels trapped,
    wants out, out, with urgency.
Receipt checked perfunctorily,
I rush the cart outside the door,
but Mom...
sits down on the floor.

And will not rise.
    Stretching out her legs,
    crossing her ankles,
she is blissfully defiant,
ignorant of the masses
bottlenecking behind her.

They glare at me.
Disdainful of my helplessness,
they think she is injured
and that I am mean.
They think I am stupid to cajole.
They offer her lifts,

and can't understand
when she resists.

I plead. I try to lead her.
I just want to leave.
I hate Costco.

Oh, floor, drop open!
Swallow me whole!
Oh, Scotty, beam me up!
Make it stop!
Cure this disease!

Kindly young nurse intercedes,
helps me hoist her,
atilt, to her feet
and walks us into the setting sun,
where Mom exclaims,
"We've been having fun!"

I still hate Costco.

For now I envy her oblivion.

I hate Costco. ❧

*The "experts" tell us, "Take the day off, you need to take
care of yourself." It's not that simple to suddenly step
out of a 24/7 caregiving life. Perhaps if caregiving didn't*

also involve emotional, psychological, and social effects in addition to physical ones, it would be remotely possible to step out of a world of isolation for a day or even a moment. It took me months to truly step out of caregiving after it was all over. Genie captures it well in her next poem.

Requiem for Monday

I can hardly wait till Monday!
Every minute of every weekend,
my friend Monday
beckons ahead.
Monday's my goal;
Monday, my salvation!

Monday is the day I'm free!
Free!
Free to get myself clean!
Free to do things for me!
Free to do my list of deeds!
Free to read, and read!

Monday, I can go outside!
Monday, I can drive!
　　drive wherever I like!
Monday, I can make my own meal!
Monday, I can eat it in peace.

Monday morning comes,
my anticipation at its peak.
I rush through Mom's ablutions.
I seat her on the bus.

Now my time arrives.
After bidding Mom bye-bye,
I re-enter our abode,
and in that very moment,
my motivation takes its leave of me.

My mind ceases its imaginings.
It becomes a desert,
lonely and dry.

I get as far as putting on the bottom sheet,
        before I wear out, sit down and stare,
        uncomprehending, at a magazine.

I start the wash, but computer-dazed,
        I ignore demands of timers beeping;
        no mere machine can animate me.

Breakfast dishes half-washed.
Linen closet doors agape.
Bathroom, toothbrush-strewn.
Watering can in repose
        part-way round the room.

One phone call maybe made,
    but my list otherwise untended.

I don't jump in the bath,
or make myself lunch.
I don't go outside,
no invigorating top-down ride.
The novel I'm into no longer appeals.

On Mondays, no friends call;
only creditors do.
They're all revving up.
Their workweek's beginning.
The only revolutions in my life
are hands circling the clock.

Cuckoo!
Unrelentingly.
Cuckoo! Cuckoo!
I am wasting the time of my life.
Cuckoo! Cuckoo! Cuckoo!
I can't wake myself up.

Cuckoo! Cuckoo! Cuckoo! Cuckoo!
Am I crazy? Or is it exhaustion?
Just pointless procrastination?
My self-exhortations don't provoke me to action –
is it a character flaw, a moral dereliction?
Or an ADD symptom?

Or depression, or both?

Cuckoo! Cuckoo! Cuckoo! Cuckoo! Cuckoo!
Now, Mom will be home
    sometime soon.
So when will I finally
    live here, too? ❧

(Maybe Wednesday.)

There are those moments of love, peace, and serenity which come when least expected in the midst of an otherwise hectic life. The wonder of this disease is that windows do open now and then, giving us moments of simple joy, gifts often taken for granted in a dementia-free household.

In a Heartbeat

It was a sunny summer afternoon
Not hot enough for air-conditioning
Yet conducive to lying around,
languorously.

Mom usually lies on her side
curled almost fetally,
as small as small as she can be.

But I found her supine atop her bed,
hands folded over her torso –

so still, and very coffin-esque.
I was about to check for breath,
when instead, her lids ascended,
pleasantly.

In the spirit of the day, I then lay
beside her, on my stomach
so our eyes could connect
for mother-daughter conversation,
the kind that's close to silent.

In the quiet of this afternoon,
occasionally riffled by a breeze,
I lay my hand upon her arm
and felt the rhythm
of our consanguinity.

I remembered summers of my Chico childhood –
How my mother took the time
to join in my languidity
and conspired with me to dream. ✿

*Holidays often leave trails of guilt and depression when
financial and physical exhaustion make it difficult to
continue traditional practices of celebration. "Live your
holidays as ordinary days" was my advice to myself
when the new millennium arrived. We sat in front of the
television set, as we had done on other holiday eves,
watching others celebrate.*

To one caregiver who felt stressed, thinking she still needed to host the traditional family Thanksgiving dinner, I suggested, "Ask your sister to take care of your mother and why don't you and your husband go see a movie?" "It was," she said, "the best Thanksgiving ever."

From a few excerpts taken from her poem "Christmas Shopping," Genie writes of such a time.

Christmas Shopping

... I wrote the date above,
twenty-third day of December,
the day I used to shop
with my own over-flowing heart
and my brain on alert
for perfect, exquisite gifts
of requisite worth.

There'll be no perfect presents this year –
just one more grocery store "splurge"
within the limits of the gift card I have left –
if I get there at all, that is –
today, or maybe tomorrow,
with Mom in tow.

I want to be jolly and ho-ho-ho,
but I dread it –
my offerings will be so paltry,
and yet they'll tap me out.

I'd like to help Mom live a little joy,
but instead I fear frustration and bother
in corralling her, not losing her
to babies and good-looking men,
or in having her poop out
in more ways than one
on the grocery store floor.

I must remind myself
that dread does not foment delight,
and I am doing the best I can.
"doing" at all is the trick;
I must do "in spite of"
to make our chance at joy. ❧

The last line in this poem tells why we are here.

What I Know

Why do you say I am sacrificing
good years of my life
for caring for my mother,
when it shouldn't be a secret
that I am really living
in a way I have never lived before?

I know I am holed-up here,
rarely venturing out,

floundering under mountains of Mom's possessions,
warehousing my profession,
eradicating my retirement,
undermining my health,
foregoing friendships, travel, restaurants,
books, and movies,
growing fatter, greyer, paler, and more wrinkled,
all while doing daily drudgery.

No, this is not sacrifice.
It is just reality.
I am really living
in a way I have never lived before.
I am living love. ❧

Eugenie Mitchell
Sacramento, California

Section II:

Two Faces of Alzheimer's Disease

What is there when poetry appears on paper, and after? There is the reality of what Alzheimer's disease is and how caregiving forces you and your loved one to live in the center of this disease. In our pursuit of using writing to understand this disease, our loved ones, and ourselves, the reality of what this disease does is not forgotten nor swept under the art of poetry or song. It forces us, along with our loved ones, to reinvent ourselves and to continuously examine what it is that we are inventing and for whom.

The 1st Face

It means BM is all over the floor or the sheets are drenched and need to be changed... again. It means caregivers gone sleepless, turning into zombies that must feed and bathe and dress their loved ones. It means caregivers on all fours, crawling from the bedroom to the kitchen to prepare meals. It means constant watching for anything out of place, for a potential fall or lethal accident waiting to happen, or for a walk outdoors turning into a 911 call.

Caregiving means transferring loved ones to a wheelchair from bed to car to ER, and waiting hours in ice-cold waiting rooms. It also means being late for medical appointments that didn't do any good anyway, or not having any medical care or health insurance available, or not having any medical help at all.

Money is running out, prescription drugs are rising in price, health services become political matters, all resulting in less and less assistance. Family members are bickering through their attorneys about loved ones' estates while their loved ones are still living. But we must protect our loved ones against all adversities, making decisions on the spot and from all corners of our caregiving world.

Reality is going to the kitchen to get your loved one a glass of water and returning to find her dead.

It means not being sure whether you're capable of conversing intelligently with anyone. Your adult conversations center on medical and disease-related issues and a television tuned to background sounds of Jeopardy and Wheel of Fortune. It is a life of isolation that numbs you, and the "self" within you is slowly disappearing. It petrifies you, knowing this "self" will reappear after caregiving, wanting life once again. Above everything else, there is that deep sense of knowing you're traveling a one-way road with no off-ramp.

All the literature on the "How To" often remain mere words when the center is shrinking smaller and smaller and there are as many different centers as there are caregivers and loved ones.

The 2nd Face

For our loved ones, what must seem at first a few strange moments, turns into an eternity of decline: the gradual disappearance of the self as a monster-sized eraser slowly sweeps the brain cells, leaving large, empty spaces. Fear and confusion replace simple uncertainties as more and more faces and objects become nameless and meaningless. Being treated as helpless and incompetent, feeling the shame of having to be so dependent, finally gives way to living in a world of bewilderment, terror, helplessness, and sadness.

Setsuko Yoshida, whose poems appeared in Mosaic Moon as a caregiver for her husband, Patrick, temporarily became the one being cared for by her son and his partner. She told me, as we sat for dinner one night in New York City where she now dwells, "The most difficult part of being cared for is the shame and the burden I have become to my son. The shame of knowing you need help in taking a bath or using the bathroom. It shames me so much to have my son see me like this. I think of how Patrick must have felt when I had to assist him with his personal functions."

This is the reality we are familiar with, and unless we are there ourselves, we will not fully understand what it's like to become dependent on others. If they could speak, perhaps this is what they would say:

Emily Dickinson, I Am Somebody

If I could speak, this is what

My voice would say:

Do not let this thief scare you away.
Do not let this thief intimidate you
Into thinking I am no longer here.

When you see me, tell me quickly who you are.
Do not ask me, "Do you know me?"
Help me retain my own dignity by not forcing me
To say, "No, I don't know who you are."
Save my face by greeting me with your name
Even if the thief has stolen all that from me.
It shames me to such indignities to know
I do not know you. Help me
In this game of pretension that the thief
Has not stolen your name from me.

My words have all forsaken me,
My thoughts are all gone. But do not
Let this thief forsake you from me.
Speak to me for I am still here.
I understand hugs and smiles and loving kindness.
When I soil my clothing or do something absurd,
Do not ask me "Why didn't you?"
If I could, I would.
I know I have turned into a monstrous baby,
If I could, I would not allow this thief
To let you live and see what he

Has stolen from me.

I know my repeated questions
Are like a record player gone bad,
But my words are gone and this is
The only way I know to make contact
With you. It is my sole way of saying,
Yes, I know you are here. This thief has stolen
Everything else except for these questions
And soon they, too, will be stolen away.

I am still here
Help me remain a human being
In this shell of a woman I have become.
In my world of silence, I am still here.
Oh, I am still here. ❧

> Frances Kakugawa
> From *Mosaic Moon*

This disease is one of the most baffling and arduous journeys both caregivers and loved ones need to muddle through so that dignity and honor can be preserved. It becomes our mission to give care to ourselves so our loved ones can in turn, receive the best from us.

... what other path is there
except the divine?
the other not taken,

would dishonor not only the woman
from whose womb I have come
but also the humanity that is mine.
what other path is there
except the divine
where love, kindness, compassion,
help me discover little pieces of myself
that make me smile,
bringing me such quiet joy
at the end of each day.
when she is gone,
the gift she gave me of myself
will bring me such sadness
but lasting peace.

From "Bless the Divine"
by Frances Kakugawa
Mosaic Moon

Section III:

Writing: Where it All Begins

an everyday miracle
of wordcrafting healing words
to caregivers of all ilk

Summer Breeze, editor
Moongate Internationale New Mexico

The process of writing forces us to make decisions about ourselves as we search for appropriate words, feelings, ideas, and thoughts, letting our true inner voice that wants to be heard, be heard.

Instead of feeling isolated and depressed or over-whelmed, the sessions made us all feel like a mis-chievous group of compatriots, a secret and special society that grew to revel in our identities as care-givers. We shared this beautiful bond of compassion and even humor in our daily tasks, and we all experi-enced profound healing.'

Jody Mishan
Caregiver from *Mosaic Moon*

Journal/Poetry Writing

How to Write a Poem

Write, write, write, I say.
But what is a poem, you ask.
And how do I write?
What can a poem hold?

It is a fragile shopping bag
   rice paper thin, egg shell thin
      but oh, don't let its appearance
         stop you from shopping.

Too heavy a load
   may rip right through and splat!
      it's all at your feet,
         or rolling into a ditch
            too shattered for all the king's men
            and all the king's horses.

There is really no way of knowing
   what weight it will hold
      or the number of items or size.

So place the content gently, slowly, into the bag.
   test it for a while, hold it close to your heart,
      swing it away to and fro, carry it a mile,
         feel it roll around the bag,

let its weight bounce against your
knees.
skip, run, walk,
and if the bag is still intact
you know the content's just about right

And what do you do with bags torn apart
and content scattered at your feet,
with no one near to give you a hand.
why, just get a truck and haul it away.

And go shopping again. ᒍ

Frances Kakugawa

You say to yourself, "But I've never written anything except emails and grocery lists. Can I write poems?" And I say, "Yes, you can."

What follows is the approach I use to help beginning writers develop their own style of writing journals and poetry in a group setting. I use it in my writing workshop for caregivers.

To set the mood for creativity, I begin by reading poems pertaining to caregiving and invite members to share their stories orally. My direct instructions to the group are printed in the non-serif, Arial font. *Background information to the leader is in square brackets. I am using a support group of caregivers as my audience, but this method can be applied to any interested group. What is missing is the laughter, tears, sharing, and feelings of camaraderie that I'm unable to reproduce here.*

First Session

[After introductions, have a brief "talk story" time to give members a chance to say why they're there and to give a short background of their caregiving situation. Read a few poems on caregiving to set the mood and to give an idea how writing is used to capture some of our most private moments in caregiving. I use poems from *Mosaic Moon* and *Breaking the Silence*.]

1. Journal writing is free writing, personal and private, so we share our writing only if we want to. Pay no attention to spelling, grammatical rules, and other writing skills. The purpose is to get your story, your feelings or thoughts, down on paper. In other words, just write. What we share in this group will be kept confidential.

2. If you're thinking, "I don't know where to begin," try this:

Thinking of the entire caregiving experience can be overwhelming. Instead of writing about the overall role of caregiving, zero in on one aspect: a feeling, a thought, or an event. Instead of writing about a whole forest of trees, go for that one blade of grass. Reach deep down into yourself at the gut level, see what's there, and write about that. What are you feeling right now? Write about that.

Setsuko Yoshida, a caregiver, wrote the following at her first session. Note the honesty and how she focused on her feelings.

Poems read by Frances Kakugawa this morning reveal the feelings of "Divine" in caregiving. How can this be? How do I reach this point in caregiving for my 84-year-old husband who is returning to child-like ways? I have such anger, resentment and frustrations at times that overwhelm me at unexpected moments throughout the day and nights. Could poetry and journal writing bring me some solace to truly see me for who I am?

3. Let's write for about 20 minutes and see where this takes us. If you'd like to go directly into poetry writing, please do so.

[I write with the group.]

[After 20 minutes of writing:]

4. Let's stop here and finish your writing at home. Who'd like to share what you've written so far?

[Feel free to make comments about what is read, encouraging each writer. Sometimes when I come across a journal entry that is compelling, shouting with a poem within, I ask for a copy. Before the next session, I lift that poem out of the journal to show how our narratives often hold beautiful poetry within them. Usually, this is all a person will need to then go on to poetry writing.]

[At one of these "first sessions," Rod Masumoto, who was sole caregiver for his mother, disproved the myth that men feel fewer emotions than women, just as Red and Jason did earlier. He wrote this after claiming, "I'm a rational man, I don't write or read poetry."]

What Do I Feel?

What do I see?
Do you see what I feel?
I feel more than you can ever see.
It hurts to feel.
I feel too, too much.
Minutes become hours,
Hours become days,
Days become years,
Years become a lifetime!
So sad to see,
So sad to feel.
I wish to feel nothing! ❧

Rod Masumoto

[Within a few weeks, Rod sent me thirty poems, written during the wee hours of the morning. His poems told a story of his own development as a caregiver son. They first questioned God, life, himself, and in this poem, acceptance.]

To My Mother

So many years ago
You gave me life
And the bond was made.
This life to see, to hear,
To taste, to touch.
But the greatest gift,
You allowed me to feel.
Through this deepest darkened night
I will hold the light
To take away all your fears.
Just know I will always be near
Through this tangled webbed maze you travel.
Have no fear, I will always be near.
I will hold this light steadfast
To make everything clear.
Just know I will always be near.
Always near, no fears. ℘

Rod Masumoto

[A year later, Rod said, "Do you know what I learned to do? I learned to put these feelings aside so I can concentrate on caring for my mother. These feelings can get in the way if I let them surface too much."

Rod didn't deny himself his emotions. He allowed himself a specific time to explore them so that he could become the rational and effective caregiver that was necessary to give the best of care to his mother. Writing became a tool to help him make sense of what he was experiencing.]

5. Continue your writing at home and we'll see you at our next session. If you'd like to share your work with me before the session, my email and telephone number are: [*provide your contact information*].

Second Session

[Begin by having caregivers share their written work since the last session. Others may want to share some of their caregiving experiences, problems, insights, etc. If you were able to lift any poems from their journals, share them now. Pass copies of the following samples out to each member to show how poems can be lifted from our narrative forms of writing. Many people may be writing in poetic form by now. They may opt to write poetry or journal entries.]

1. If you'd like to try poetry writing, look at the journal entry Sets Yoshida wrote at the first session. The accompanying poem is taken from her journal. None of her own words were changed except for the deletion of a few words and the rearrangement of certain lines. In poetry, we say things as precisely as we can to capture the essence of what we want to say.

> Poems read by Frances Kakugawa this morning reveal the feelings of "Divine" in caregiving. How can this be? How do I reach this point in caregiving for my 84-year-old husband who is returning to child-like ways? I have such anger, resentment and frustrations at times that overwhelm me at unexpected moments throughout the day and nights. Could

poetry and journal writing bring me some solace to
truly see me for who I am?

Now look at the following poem structured from her writing:

Can I?

Poems by Frances this morning
Reveal the feelings of "divine"
In caregiving.

How can this be?
Can I, too, reach this point
In caring for my 84-year-old husband
Who is returning to childlike ways?

Anger, resentment and frustrations
Overwhelm me at unexpected moments
Throughout the days and nights.

How can I deal with such thoughts and feelings?
Can poetry and journal writing bring me some solace
To truly see me for who I am? ❧

Setsuko Yoshida
from *Mosaic Moon*

2. The next journal entry describes a morning when I was
driving my mother to her day care center. A poem, "The Red
Umbrella," was "lifted" from this journal entry.

I was stuck in traffic with my mother at my side near
an overpass. I was stuck in more ways than one.
We sat in the car, her voice repeating over and over,
"Where am I going?" I sat and watched a woman
walk across the overpass, carrying a black umbrella.
I sat there and thought, "Now if that woman had
a red umbrella, it would create a lovelier image.
Red against that blue sky. Better yet, if a child was
walking with that umbrella, I would see only the red
umbrella walking." These thoughts took the edge off
the traffic jam, the looming high-rises and my mother's repetitive voice of concern. I soon continued my
drive to adult day care.

A Red Umbrella

A red umbrella
Moves across the overpass.
I smile as I sit
In traffic below.
Is it a child
Late for school
Or did Mary Poppins
Get lost in flight?
Such frivolous thoughts
As I drive my mother
To adult day care. ৶

3. Note the poetic license I took in recreating some of the
images to empower the poem. Also note how I went for that one

blade of grass, the red umbrella. There were high-rise buildings, traffic, noise, my mother next to me asking over and over again, "Where are we going?" I stayed with the red umbrella image. We often need to create images beyond what our senses have seen, heard, touched, felt, or smelled to enhance our writing.

[Once again, spend the rest of the session on writing poetry or journal entries.]

Ongoing Sessions

[Continue to meet, talk stories, write, and share writings and experiences.]

The following were observed or expressed in my support group as time went on:

- ❀ Hearing others speak of their experiences gave us permission to be honest and unashamed of any of our feelings and perceptions.

- ❀ The tears, laughter, and teasing began to bond us at a spiritual level and we began to truly understand what human dignity and love were all about as we began rising above the burden of caregiving. We remained individuals but also became part of a whole. Most importantly, we felt we were not alone, our plight was understood and our loved ones were receiving the best possible care with love and compassion.

- ❀ This relationship that developed in the group also expanded outside of our sessions. We were there for

each other at hospitals, funeral parlors and made
numerous home visits so our loved ones became part
of our group.

Most importantly, the relationship between caregivers and
their loved ones began to transform into one of greater depth
of love and commitment. As one woman announced during
the first session, "I can hardly wait to go home to love my
father." Or as another caregiver emailed me, "Thank you for
bringing writing into my life. What a difference it's making
in my caring for my mother."

Yes, writing makes a difference. One morning, I walked
into my mother's bathroom and found BM all over the floor.
In my panicked state of experiencing this for the first time
(things do get easier, almost to a way of life after a while), I
grabbed my toothbrush and soon found myself on my hands
and knees, scrubbing bathroom tiles.

The hilarity of this image instantly turned me into a poet.
I began to pay attention to what I was doing, thinking to
myself, "Hmmm, maybe there's a poem here." The moment I
thought "poem," I was no longer a suffering caregiver cleaning up BM but I was a poet/caregiver, creating an art form.
This poem is a result of that poetic morning:

A Feather Boa and a Toothbrush

It is 3 a.m.
I am on my hands and knees
With toothbrush in one hand,
A glass of hot water in my other,
Scrubbing BM off my mother's

Bathroom floor.

Before a flicker of self pity can set in,
A vivid image enters my mind.
An image of a scarlet feather boa
Impulsively bought from Neiman Marcus,
Delicately wrapped in white tissue
Awaiting in my cedar chest
For some enchanting evening.
The contrast between my illusionary lifestyle
Of feather boas, Opium perfume and black velvet
And my own reality of toothbrushes
Bathroom tiles and BM at 3 a.m.
Overwhelms me with silent laughter. ♫

> From: *Mosaic Moon: Caregiving Through Poetry*
> By Frances H. Kakugawa

Helpful Hints

As we began to transform from over-burdened caregivers to poet-caregivers, our writing, too, began to reveal this transformation. The following practices aided us in finding more successful and skillful ways of using language for our purposes:

- ❀ Have copies of poems available. Often they became models for discussion and helped to expand our knowledge of other concrete forms and uses of language.

❀   Read poems aloud to check for rhythm, tone, and sound. This led to editing: replacing a word or words or rearranging lines to smooth out the rhythm and sound of each poem. Often a person reading her or his poem aloud edits as the reading continues.

❀   Experience other published works of poets. Members brought in poems of other poets. This exposure to other writers' use of language added to our knowledge. Seeing how different authors make language work for them helps to develop one's own style of writing.

Literary Elements and Devices

Yes, we are not here to write the best of poems for any contest or publication, but merely to tell our stories. However, I have found that awareness of a few literary elements and devices gives writers tools for using language more effectively for what they want to say.

When appropriate, point out some of the basic devices and elements found in their poems or journal entries. Mention how their use of language created images, metaphors, symbols, and other techniques writers often use. Discuss the following language devices and techniques as they appear in their writings instead of turning the session into a writing-skills classroom. The examples are taken from the works in this book.

Imagery: The images that language creates in our minds. The more detailed and descriptive the images, the more successful and powerful the writing. For example:

> "She tied that bow with such perfect concentration, pulling the loop around the index, saddling the bitter end, done at last, when she coaxed the lace over the arthritic arch of her bony finger." Red (page 106)

Simile: Two objects or entities are compared, using "like" or "as" as connectives. For example:

> "Life for them must have been so fragile, precious but tenuous, like a silk thread." Jason (page 70)

Metaphor: Unlike similes, we suggest one thing *is* the other. In my last poem in this book, I use a shopping bag as the metaphor for a poem.

> "It is a fragile shopping bag, rice paper thin, egg shell thin," Frances (page 145)

Another example is:

> "I am the *torero*," Eugenie (page 117)

Symbol: Often a concrete or real object is used to represent an idea. Wings, for example, are often used as a symbol for freedom.

> "I am generations of women waiting to be dragonfly wings." Frances (page 18)

Allusion: A reference is made to a well-known person, place, thing, or event that is assumed to be familiar to the reader.

This first example refers to Dian Fossey's work with gorillas.

> "But the eyes, like the incomparable wells of pathos and curiosity Dian Fossey once recorded in the faces of another species." Red (page 103)

The next example refers to Thomas Wolfe's book *You Can't Go Home Again.*

> "Going Home with Thomas Wolfe." Frances (page 8)

This third example alludes to the windmills in *Don Quixote.*

> "Alzheimer's leaves me tilting at windmills." Linda (page 81)

Alliteration: Words with similar consonant sounds at the beginning are repeated in a line or lines. Note the sound of "s" in the following example:

> "She suddenly squeezes my side at the waist." Elaine (page 58)

Once again, we are not writing for literary prizes or for professional editors. We are merely using written or oral language in journals or poetry, to tell our stories and to preserve memories which would otherwise be lost, and to help us make sense of what's going on in our lives. To quote Sets Yoshida from *Mosaic Moon:*

> When Frances said the source of writing is myself, and that once I release my poem to others, it no longer belongs to me, I found this to be very helpful

in letting go of my negative feelings. Writing releases my burden, and the creative process and the poem form a balanced perspective in the healing and transforming of the burden I carry. This returns me to my caregiving with love, compassion and understanding.

Writing in Other Areas

This basic approach to journal and poetry writing can be applied to any support group of varied interests or to individuals who wish to work alone. The following poems were written privately during two periods in my life. The writing process brought the same comfort, insights, emotional and psychological growth and artistic gratification as it did when providing care for my mother.

Cancer?

"We need a biopsy,"
He matter-of-factly tells me,
Looking at me straight into the eyes.
"It may be cancer."
Cancer? How dare you say
Cancer.
Why not something
Vague and unclear like
"Unforeseen cell growth" or
Why not even,
"There's probably nothing wrong with you
But we'll take tests anyway."

Damn you! How dare you say
Cancer
And look me
Straight in the eye.
Lie to me, you bastard!
He is waiting for me to speak.
I say nothing.
I look him straight
In the eye.
Cancer? ✽

Prognosis: Cancer

Like lightning bolt,
He sizzles d-e-a-t-h
Upon my back.
    Why didn't you lie
    When I said
    I wanted the truth?
The Artist
In his Gallery
Pinpoints
My imperfection
On the screen.
    Are you sure
    You know my name?
A statistician
Drops a number
Into my womb.

If I smile
Will he wake me
From this lie?
The Arctic Wind
It chills and freezes.
 Fire to Ice.
 I promise to be good.
 I don't want to die.
Ice. ☙

Surgery

As the white knights
Gather around me
I think with sadness:
 If I should die
 No one in this immaculate room
 Would shed half a tear
 For me.
 My heart, lungs,
 And uterus
 Are as anonymous
 As a faceless stranger
 In a crowd.
 They cannot hear
 My rage against
 This anonymity.
 Ah, I did rage
 Against the black
 Night. ☙

Where Are The Pretty Thoughts?

"This will sting you a little"
The anesthesiologist quietly and soothingly says.
"This will make you somewhat drowsy."
Slowly I begin to lose consciousness.
How many times a day has he said that to patients
Who tensely hear it for the first time?
I open my eyes, heavy with sleep
The ceiling waves above me.
Thoughts of dying
Enter my mind.
"I may never come out of this,"
I panic and find
Breathing not so natural.
My insides begin to tremble.
The trembling slowly crawls outside of my skin
To my arms and inner thighs.
God, I'm so terribly alone and frightened.
Who can help me?
Think pretty thoughts, I tell myself.
Pretty thoughts. What are pretty thoughts?
Meadows with brooks? Birds? Flowers?
Christmas. Yes, Christmas.
The trees go on sale tomorrow.
My students, perhaps. Let me see their faces.
What are pretty thoughts
When dying is real?
The tightening gets tighter.

The chilling and trembling continue.
Can I ask them to stop? Yes, I'll ask them to stop.
Another shot of anesthesia.
I hear muffled voices of
The White Knights around the
Cold, rectangular table.
Where are my pretty thoughts?
What can they be?
Am I going to die? ◢⅋

The Verdict

He looks me straight
In the eye.
I know that look.
"There's no malignancy."
I look him straight
In the eye.
And say nothing. ◢⅋

Here, I walk through my fear inch by inch, similar to working on a jigsaw puzzle, beginning with all the scattered pieces to the gradual formation of the whole.

Jigsaw Puzzle

in total chaos
  a thousand piece spread
    overturned, strewn, piece upon piece,
      senseless, meaningless,
        no magical code to make them
          whole
            except for the fitting of piece
            unto piece.

the formation of the border,
  the first glimmer of hope,
    while in the center,
      a mountainous mass
        saved for the coming
          of the final score.

fingers searching, pushing, forcing
  piece unto piece for a whole among parts.
    the curvatures small for a clutching fit.
      the turning, twisting, tossing trials
        for one sudden fit of a connecting
          cry.
            sometimes, a fit irrationally
            found
              just by staring at one
              tiny piece.

edge against edge, mounts into shape;
piece unto piece, the center grows
from border to mass, a disappearing space,
the external shine bruised by handling.
a final whole after the parts
by one tiny piece of insignificant form
snugly pushed for the resurrected whole.   ✣

From *The Path of Butterflies*
by Frances H. Kakugawa

Conclusion

It seems only fitting that the last voice comes from a loved one who had Alzheimer's Disease. With the spirit of my mother, I recreated this voice with help from Red Slider. Once again, the thief fails each time the lives of our loved ones are preserved and memorialized through the arts, story-telling, and daily reflections.

Hey Alzheimer's

Hey Alzheimer's,
Sitting there so smug, gloating
Over the memories
You have stolen, the years we have lost.
Do I have a story to tell you.

You see, Alzheimer's,
What you think you took, we kept.
Every memory we secreted away
In our children, our friends,
Our loved ones.

You could not rob us, though we forgot.
You could not erase us, though we could not write.
You could not silence, though we could not speak.
The stories, the laughter, the moments that passed
Into their keep, you could not steal
Into a night of silence.

Look at me, Alzheimer's.
My life is restored, remembered, reconstructed,
With tools of love, dignity and laughter.
A house of memories is built
By my children, and their children
For generations to come.

So here I am, Alzheimer's,
With family, friends, and loved ones.
What you thought you stole
Is still here. We are all still here.
So Alzheimer's,
What do you think of that?

> Written in tribute to "Doc Buyers" of
> Hawai'i and to all our loved ones.

In conclusion, there is no one cardinal rule for writing as there is no one way to give care. Each must discover his or her own style and genre of writing and this process begins by being true to oneself.

Frances H. Kakugawa

Suggested Resources

Creech, Sharon. *Love that Dog*, HarperCollins Publishers, New York, 2001. A delightful children's story about a boy who believes boys don't write poetry and ends up being a poet. His thoughts are presented in journal-poetic form. A must-read.

Fletcher, Ralph. *A Writer's Notebook: Unlocking the Writer Within You*, Avon books, Inc. New York, 1996. A guide that shows you how to keep a writer's notebook with entries that can lead to poems, stories, etc.

Kakugawa, Frances H. *Mosaic Moon: Caregiving Through Poetry*, Watermark Publishing, Honolulu, Hawai'i, 2002. A collection of poems written by caregivers who were members of the author's first writing support group for caregivers.

Kakugawa, Frances H. *Wordsworth Dances the Waltz*, Watermark Publishing, Honolulu, Hawai'i, 2007. An award-winning illustrated children's story of Wordsworth, a poet mouse, who writes poems to help him understand why his grandmother is being treated differently due to the changes brought about by aging. His poems help his parents realize she is still a person even in her dementia state.

Kooser, Ted, and Steve Cox. *Writing Brave & Free*,
University of Nebraska Press, Lincoln, Nebraska,
2006. This writer-friendly book by the U.S. Poet
Laureate takes readers from rough drafts to revised,
final copies. The author strongly suggests the journal
is the best place to practice writing brave and free.
You'll smile at one unit title, "We Don't Need No
Stinkin' Rules."

Kooser, Ted. *The Poetry Home Repair Manual*, University
of Nebraska Press, Lincoln, Nebraska, 2007. A
handbook that supports developing and practicing
poets on the craft of writing poetry. You'll feel you're
in the same room with the kind and gentle instructor.

If after all this you still feel the need for a guiding hand
to help you get started, I extend my own to you. I can be
reached in care of the publisher or at my blog or website:

Frances Kakugawa at:

www.francesk.org.

http://franceskakugawa.wordpress.com

Willow Valley Press at:

http://www.btsilence.com

http://www.willowvalleypress.com